The Mystery of Communion

The Mystery of Communion
Encountering the Trinity
GIULIO MASPERO
PRESENTED BY JOHN C. CAVADINI
TRANSLATED BY COLIN HOWELL

ST. AUGUSTINE'S PRESS
South Bend, Indiana

Library of Congress Control Number: 2020952410

∞ The paper used in this publication meets the minimum requirements of the American National Standard for Information Sciences – Permanence of Paper for Printed Materials, ANSI Z39.48-1984.

St. Augustine's Press
www.staugustine.net

Table of Contents

Presentation   vii
Preface   xii
Introduction   1
1. The Word of the God of the Covenant   6
2. The Word of the Triune God: Jesus   15
3. The Response to the Word: The Faith of the Church   28
4. The Development of Thought: Theology   61
5. The Trinitarian View of Man and the World   81
6. Conclusion: Mary and the Trinity   101

Presentation

"For the Son of Man came not to be served, but to serve, and to give his life as a ransom for many" (Mk 10:45). Thus does Jesus describe his vocation. But what is the significance of this gift of his own life? Whose self-gift is it, when the "Son of Man" gives his life for the many? Who is the Son of Man?

Obviously this is the title of a human being. True, it is rich with prophetic resonance from its echoing the language of the Book of Ezekiel, and it is endowed with apocalyptic urgency from its echoing of the Book of Daniel. Yet we see in the Gospel of Mark how utterly human is "the Son of Man", and how recognizable his humanity is as our own. We see him baptized, seemingly like any other sinner (Mk 1:4, 9) even though he hears the voice from heaven proclaiming him God's beloved Son, and the Spirit descending upon him like a dove (Mk 1:10–11). We see him feel compassion at the hungry crowd (Mk 8:2). We see him "distressed and troubled," his soul "very sorrowful, even to death" (14:34), and in his desolation, we see him pray to the Father three times, only to be betrayed and abandoned, not only by Judas and the disciples, but, as he himself cries out, by God Himself (16:34).

Yet there is more to the story. Whose self-gift is described in these passages? We have seen that it is the self-gift of a human being, recognizable in the desolation to which his gift of himself as a servant has led him. And yet the Gospel does not allow the question to rest there. The reader can't help but wonder, or at least contemplate the question, why is he praying for help? Haven't we who have been reading the Gospel, seen him feed the multitudes miraculously, cure the sick and make the blind see? Haven't we seen him raise the dead? Haven't we seen him order the elements, the wind and the waves, to be still? "Who then is this, that even wind and sea obey him?" (Mk 4:41). Good question, intended for the reader to ponder. If the reader knows the Scriptures, he or she will hear the "echo," as Richard Hays puts it, of Ps 107:23–30, which describes God's commanding the "stormy wind" and the "waves of the sea" (Ps 107:25), both to rouse them and to calm them. Perhaps the reader will remember as well that of all of Jesus's miracles, this one alone, the commanding of the wind and the waves, is reserved to God Himself in the Scriptures. Even Elijah and Elisha raise the dead. So the question is not asked, "Who then is this who raises the dead," but rather and precisely, "Who then is this, that even wind and sea obey him?"

The answer, it is implied by the echo of the Scriptures, is "God." In some unthinkable, unimaginable way, the Son of Man is divine, as evidenced by the fact that he has all of the divine power at his disposal without having to ask and without evident assistance (such as God driving the sea back when Moses stretches out his hand over it, Ex 15:21). But then, the Agony in the Garden is whose agony? Whose self-gift? Somehow, the Gospel is telling us, that in this very human self-gift is also in some way nothing less than God's self-gift! But how can God bend down so low as to be in such desolation that, like us, he prays for a miracle? And doesn't even get it! How can God pray? To whom is He praying? It is not true prayer if it is not directed to God. And yet, if God can pray to Himself, how is that true prayer? None of us have the luxury of praying to ourselves! One is not very desolate if one can pray to oneself, since one is sure to be heard!

So we see how the Gospel brings the Trinitarian question into focus as precisely a question about how God can be so loving that He can bend down far enough to actually pray and have it be true prayer. He has to be praying to the same *thing* that He is, that is, to someone whose *nature* or *essence* is divine, and yet, He can't be praying to Himself but must be praying to **someone** *else*, to another—we have to find language—*person*, is the word chosen. The Gospel presents "the mystery from which all true love flows," as Prof. Maspero puts it, but in the story and narrative form of the evangelical proclamation, it is of course without the technical language that was developed later. But we see here revealed the mystery of a God who loves so much that he can "empty himself" (to use the words of Phil 2:7) to take on a true human existence, true enough to allow for true prayer that is not play-acting of some sort. The mystery of the Trinity is the mystery of the God who can act with this degree of love, such that the gift of the Son of Man's life for the ransom of many, is at one and the same time the self-gift of God Himself, self-emptied utterly even into our desolation, for the ransom of many.

What Prof. Maspero shows us, as he makes his careful way through the developments of the Trinitarian language and doctrine, is that the language and doctrine is developed *not* to overlay the fundamental biblical proclamation of the God of love whose mystery is so great that He could empty Himself to the point of praying, as though the doctrine were cluttering this primordial biblical proclamation with useless technical supplements, "rationalizing" the mystery and thereby blocking the encounter with this God to which Scripture invites us—but rather just the opposite. He shows how the language is developed to *preserve* the mystery of God the Trinity as the "mystery from which all true love flows," just as the Word of God in Scripture and Tradition proclaim it. He shows how the development of the language of essence (or substance, in Latin), hypostasis (or person), and of the notion of relations of origin as that alone in which the persons are distinct from each other (as opposed to a distinction in the one nature), uses philosophical language in such a way that it is contoured to the revealed mystery, rather than contouring the revealed mystery to itself and thus reducing it to merely a truth of human reason.

For example, to take the terms in which I set out—*whose* self-gift is it when the Son of Man gives his life as a ransom for many? It is both a human self-gift and God's self-gift. But how? If God empties Himself to accept the form of a servant to serve rather than to be served, is it a "part" of God that is emptied? Is "part of God," called "the Father" by the Gospel, left in Heaven, and part of God, called the "Son" by the Gospel, on earth? But the Gospel shows us an utterly unreserved and unconstrained self-gift, with nothing held back, to the point where the one who can command the wind and the waves allows Himself to be betrayed, taken, arrested and abandoned. This is no partial gift with reservations. The doctrine of the Trinity, as Prof. Maspero leads us through it, shows us how the idea of relation of origin makes it so that, when the Word becomes flesh, *all* of God becomes flesh—there is no "God" leftover or held back—and that is in turn because, when the Father begets the Son (which is from all eternity), His self-emptying in love is so complete that there is no "God," no divinity or divine substance, left over. That is how the Father is Father and the Son is perfect image, because there is no holding back of anything in His generation. And, when the Son gives Himself back in obedience to the Father, there is no God left over, no divinity not offered back, and this is how the Son is Son and, once again, perfect image of the Father. And the Holy Spirit is the love they share, not a "part" of God's substance but all of it, so self-emptying is the Love that unites Father and Son.

Thus Prof. Maspero shows the reader not only *what* the Trinitarian doctrine is, but *why it matters*, and, in particular, why it matters to speak in theologically precise terms not only when engaged in theology proper, but when engaged in catechesis and in preaching. Perhaps there is no doctrine less well taught or less well preached than the doctrine of the Trinity. Prof. Maspero's excellent treatment provides a theologically precise account of the doctrine of the Trinity that is ordered and articulated in such a way that it is also catechetically useful. It provides the crucial distinctions as each of them developed, and thus helps the reader not only to master the distinctions but also to learn *why they matter*. What we lose when we lose sight of these distinctions, teach them imprecisely or preach in a way that downplays them, is nothing less than the deepest of all biblical truths, namely, that God is Love, and that in revelation we find proclaimed a love so wondrous and so unimaginable that, while it welcomes the categories of reason to help articulate an "understanding" of it, it also shatters the very categories as it uses them.

For that reason, as well as many others, such as its very learned character, which nevertheless does not call attention to itself as such and therefore seems (and is!) very approachable, I am very happy to be able to "present" this book to an English speaking audience, and to warmly welcome Prof. Maspero into our language, where I know his work will be just as valuable as it has been in its original Italian. I predict that this book will find its way into many different venues, classrooms and studies, where theological scholarship and pastoral effectiveness are both, and equally, prized.

John C. Cavadini
Department of Theology, University of Notre Dame and Director of the McGrath Institute for Church Life

Preface

A few years ago, I was invited to a Jewish literature festival to talk about the importance of work and rest from a biblical perspective. I planned prior to this to talk to the Chief Rabbi of Rome and tried to prepare myself as much as possible. Before becoming a priest and devoting myself to theology I worked as a physicist, collaborating with several Russian Jews who came to Europe immediately after the fall of the Berlin Wall, and for this I am well aware of their seriousness. When, after the rabbi spoke, I was given the floor, I foolishly began my speech with the name of God—that is, I used the revealed Name that out of profound reverence the Jews do not pronounce. It would be like inviting the representative of another religion to speak to a Christian community, only to hear him pronounce blasphemy.

At the end of the meeting I rushed to apologize to the rabbi, and he told me that he had spoken about this problem (typical of Christian theologians) with Joseph Ratzinger, then Pope Benedict XVI. He lamented that a scientific approach to theology might lead one to forget that the Bible is alive, that it involves the lives of real people in the past, but also in the present, and that only from this perspective can one grasp its message. From this moment the idea of a written introduction to the Trinity and how to approach it was born in me, something that might draw specialists and laypersons alike deeper into the mystery.

This book, then, serves as a brief introduction to the study of the Triune God. It is a narrative designed to highlight the most important points in the development of Trinitarian thought, with an emphasis on how classical metaphysics was modified in the wake of the revealed truths and how this could be relevant for our postmodern times. A renewed ontology emerges, one that acknowledges the original role of relation joined with essence. The intention is to help fill in the gaps of thought that Benedict XVI addresses in his encyclical *Caritas in Veritate,* where he calls for a more thorough treatment of the metaphysics of the interpersonal relationship (n. 53).

This can also help us to better understand the Magisterium of Pope Francis, who often refers to the teaching of St. John Paul II on the Trinitarian foundation of the family. In the *Amoris Laetitia* he says: "With a gaze of faith and love, grace and fidelity, we have contemplated the relationship between human families and the divine Trinity. The word of God tells us that the family is entrusted to a man, a woman and their children, so that they may become a communion of persons in the image of the union of the Father, the Son and the Holy Spirit. Begetting and raising children, for its part, mirrors God's creative work. The family is called to join in daily prayer, to read the word of God and to share in Eucharistic communion, and thus to grow in love and become ever more fully a temple in which the Spirit dwells" (n. 29).

The present volume is written in a concise and accessible format with only necessary textual references cited. Ideally, one should study this book alongside Holy Scripture, referring back to the passages indicated herein. For further reading on the subject one should consult the proper textbook, *The Mystery of the Triune God* (L.F. Mateo-Seco, G. Maspero). The structure of this textbook is very similar to what the reader will find in the present work. Other valuable sources are two succinct and invaluable books that I highly recommend: J. Ratzinger, *The God of Jesus Christ: Meditations on God in the Trinity* (Chicago: Franciscan Herald Press, 1979) and

J. Daniélou, *God's Life in Us* (Denville, NJ: Dimension Books, 1969).

My hope for the reader is that this little book may help him discover that the Trinity really is "the mystery from which all true love flows" (Pope Francis, *Amoris Laetitia*, n. 63).

Introduction

Recently I was telling a philosopher friend about my studies on the Trinity when he said, "Clearly, God is one *in spite of being* three Persons." The truth of this statement struck me. It seems wholly contradictory that God is really one *and* three. Another reflection began to take form—God is truly one *exactly because* He is three. The transition from "*in spite of being*" to "*precisely because*" is not trivial: It is the result of an incredible, wonderful history, one that has seen the dawning and development of an authentically Christian thought, sparked and ignited by the revelation of the Trinity in Jesus Christ.

This little book provides a brief sketch of this history. It shows how from the concept of unity that characterized classical philosophy and was molded through the observation of nature, our understanding has gradually matured and deepened to a degree that humanity could never have grasped on its own. This kind of perception was only possible because of God's self-revelation of His immanence, that is His heart and His "within". The revelation of His being wholly and eternally Father and Son and the Love between Them has made a more complete, fuller *unity* known to humanity—the perfect unity of divine communion. The very foundation of being, the absolute reality—which is the basis of all other reality—is indeed communion of love, personal unity that is given *in* relation and not *in spite of* relation. This is truly a novel concept, an extension of Greek philosophy, through the new value assigned to communion and relation.

Revelation obviously changes the methodological approach to

the mystery of God because this mystery is no longer known exclusively through the categories formulated by the observation of nature. The Incarnation opens humanity to this radically novel concept which would have been otherwise impossible for us to conceive. The human person, being made in the image and likeness of the Creator, becomes a privileged path of relationship with God, so much so that, in the Incarnation, God gives Himself to us in the Man who is Christ—a man with a mother, a family, a story, friends and a job.

Common knowledge tells us that it is simpler to know a stone or a tree than another person, for no human being can be reduced to mere externals, ignoring interior elements like human freedom. Human existence can certainly be observed from an external perspective, yet to *know* another person truly one needs to enter into relation and share intimacy. One might say that every person is a *mystery,* where by '*mystery*' we do not mean the same thing as in a detective novel or in natural science. There, the word *mystery* is more like a question with a precise answer (i.e. *who* is the murderer? What is the result of a certain equation?), and the difficulty in unveiling the answer is only due to the limits of our cognitive ability. In these cases, the mystery is like a veil that masks the object to be known, something too burdensome and heavy to lift, but one could lift it with sufficient strength. Instead, the mystery who is a person—that is, an authentic mystery—does not consist of a solution of a mathematical problem and is not to be found in the answer to a riddle. In a strict sense, one might say that this mystery cannot even be *un-veiled,* as when we discover the answers to a crossword puzzle. Rather, this mystery, this person *re-veals* himself, lets himself be known. In fact, with each advance of this kind of personal knowledge, every lifting of a veil implies the discovery of an underlying reality which is shrouded by yet another veil. We go deeper and deeper from veil to veil. This is what one means by *revelation,* for the mystery of the person possesses an infinite depth that can never be fully exhausted.

The most precious realities, all those of truly great value, belong to this second type of mystery. So, *a fortiori*, this is the context in which God must be placed. Indeed, as Joseph Ratzinger writes, God is the ultimate reason for the existence of this mystery:

> We cannot overlook the fact that we are now touching a realm in which Christian theology must be more aware of its limits than it has often been in the past; a realm in which any falsely-directed attempt to gain too precise a knowledge is bound to end in disastrous foolishness; a realm in which only the humble admission of ignorance can be true knowledge and only wondering attendance before the incomprehensible mystery can be the right confession of faith in God. Love is always *mysterium*—more than one can reckon or grasp by subsequent reckoning. Love itself—the uncreated, eternal God—must therefore be in the highest degree a mystery—"the *mysterium* itself."[1]

In technical terms, the impossibility of speaking of God unless in the face of His infinite greatness is what is known as *apophaticism*. Reason may come to demonstrate His existence, but the mystery of God's immanence, the inner-life of the three Persons and their mutual and eternal relations, exists beyond all human capacity of expression. A medieval legend illustrates this when it describes Augustine's encounter with a child on the seashore where the child was drawing water from the ocean to pour it into a hole in the sand. As the saint stood nearby and was clearly perplexed by this activity, the child remarked that it would be easier to empty the sea than to understand the Trinity through human reason. By

---

1   (J. Ratzinger, *Introduction to Christianity*, San Francisco: Ignatius Press, 1990, 114).

analogy, this brings to mind the beautiful verse of Rabindranath Tagore:

> Water in a vessel shimmers,
> water in the sea obscure.
> Small truth speaks in words that are clear,
> great truth bears great silence.

With the Incarnation, God revealed Himself to us as Father, Son and Holy Spirit, forcing man to a radical re-examination of his conception of God and reality. The natural categories are thereby reformulated in the light of the Gospel. Old concepts are re-clothed in new meaning. Thus emerge the merits of a kind of thought designed to facilitate an encounter with the Christian God. Truth is identified with Christ and the Trinity, and hence is found in the personal dimension, such that the doctrine of the Trinity can never take the place of the Trinity itself. Yet just as in the case of a map needed for a journey, the cognitive content prevents us from getting lost, keeps us from reducing and simplifying the Trinity into something we understand only on a natural level. The value of the map is merely this—it leads us into the place that is reproduced on paper only schematically. It links us to reality.

Thus, Trinitarian theology helps us enter into relation with the Trinity Itself, following in the footsteps of the woman who first opened Herself to this kind of thought: Mary.[2]

---

2 Explaining her title as the Mother of God (*Theotókos* in Greek), Benedict XVI has summed up the novelty of this path admirably: "Aristotelian philosophy, as we well know, tells us that between God and man there exists only a non-mutual relation. Man relates to God, but God, the Eternal, is in himself and does not change: He cannot have one relation today and another tomorrow. He exists within himself and not in relation with something outside of him. This is a very logical message but a message that causes us to despair: As a result of it, God himself is not in relation with me. With the

Incarnation, with the coming of the *Theotókos*, this changed radically because God drew us into himself and *is* relation within himself. He really has created relation with us. In that moment, God wanted to be born from a woman and always be himself: This is the great event." (Benedict XVI, 11 October 2010, *Meditations During the First General Congregation of the Special Assembly for the Middle East of the Synod of Bishops*).

1. The Word of the God of the Covenant

The stages of the encounter

The development of the conceptions about God runs parallel to the history of Israel and the formation of its identity within a constitutive relationship with God Himself. This progression can be sketched in five stages in which the emphasis is placed on the conceptual and theological distinctions rather than the chronological sequence and historical-critical approach.

1, *From a clan to a people.* Primitive religions held divinities to be, essentially, personifications of natural forces. For example, all ancient pagan cultures claimed the existence of a god of the sky or a god of the sea and of rivers. There was a multiplicity of gods, all organised hierarchically according to the outcome of their wars with one another. Mountains and all high ground became associated with them as their homes. Inhabitants of particular territories worshiped these various divinities, paying homage to them through sacrifices intended to win their favour.

The Hebrew tribes were initially a nomadic people and claimed no territory of their own. Indeed, this lack of placement implied that they were obliged to pay a form of homage to all the gods of the territories they passed through in search of pastures for their cattle.

The unification of these tribes into one people was a result of their encounter with God, the Creator of heaven and earth. The identity of Israel developed through this dialogue with a God who is not a mere natural force but the God who is a person and pursues human beings and speaks to them. The fact that God enters into relation with them is not a sign of weakness. Rather it is a mark of the omnipotence of the One who is the Creator. In fact, His power extends to every territory and He can defend the clan wherever they go. The God of Israel is the most powerful of all gods. He is, indeed, so powerful that He can literally draw near and enter into relation with these people. While still without a name, this God is nonetheless, and significantly, identified as the God of their fathers (*Gen* 31:5, 50:17; *Ex* 3:6, 18:4). He is identified as the God whom their ancestors had known and whom they even held in friendship. Israel's very identity is based, then, on its relation to God, a relation that is expressed in the vertical Covenant between Him and His people. This vertical Covenant also served as the source of the horizontal covenants that existed between the various tribes who were thereby rendered capable of a kind of unity which had previously been unimaginable.

This is the first phase in a history marked by both light and shade. From its very beginning, it is characterized by a unique conception of God. All the ancient pagan cultures held fast to the notion that the cosmos and likewise their own identity emerged from a kind of divine conflict, that is, a struggle between the gods, as between a positive and negative first principle. For Israel alone, there is a sole good principle who is the ultimate origin of all that *is* in that He is the Creator of it all. He is a personal God, intimately close to humanity and yet He is also, at the same time, utterly transcendent, that is, above both nature and the people.

2. *The revelation of the name.* The uniqueness of the Hebrew conception of God is reinforced by the second period of this history, culminating in the stable settlement in the Promised Land, and is realized precisely through the covenant with Yahweh. Israel now ceases to be a nomadic people. Prior to this all renunciation

of the worship of local gods only implied some kind of covenant with this Creator, but now this is made explicit and ratified in an official capacity. God treats man as an equal and has dealings with him. With Moses, He goes so far as to reveal His name (*Ex* 3:14). This is a critical moment because, in a certain sense, God offers even more of Himself in the relationship with His people through the revelation of His own name, something which affords the possibility of constant contact with Him. The way in which the dialogue between Moses and God unfolds on Mount Horeb is iconic (*Ex* 3:13–15). Before God tells Moses to bring the people of Israel out of the land of Egypt, Moses, true to his culture, begins to "negotiate" with God, asking for some sort of guarantee—such as His name—so that the people will believe and follow him. The answer "I am who I am" indicates the proper name of the God whom Abraham, Isaac, and Jacob had all known: "I am," as transcribed in the sacred tetragram, *Yahweh*. In the Semitic languages, the generic term indicating divinity—and therefore also the false gods—is *El* with its plural form *Elohim* which is used in the same way, even if it was more often used as a *plural of majesty* to indicate the supreme God and thereby the true God. Yahweh, on the other hand, is a personal name with origins connected with the verb *to be*, rendering it susceptible of various interpretations.

God's response to Moses could certainly be viewed as *evasive* in the sense that "I am who I am" is akin to giving no response at all—affirming His absolute sovereignty as in the similar formula, "I the Lord will speak the word that I speak" (*Ezek* 12:25). At the same time, however, the Hebrew expression can also be read in the future tense as, "I shall be Whom I shall be," demonstrating God's promise to remain close throughout the crossing of the desert. It is as though God were saying to Moses: "Go tell the Israelites that my identity is that of *being* so great that I can be with them wherever they go; my person is *ever-present* to protect and safeguard." Thus, the name also indicates *efficacy* and fidelity.

Lastly, in the Greek translation of the Old Testament known as the Septuagint—which emerged in Alexandria between the third and second centuries B.C.—the term "I am" is rendered in perfect parallel with the Platonic formula indicating Being as First Principle. There is, then, a third and *ontological* interpretation, which clearly transcends the confines of the Semitic culture by identifying the God of Israel with that of the philosophers in a metaphysical way.

3. *The kingdom of Israel.* The third stage in the progressive understanding of God in Israel is characterized by the fact that the conception of the one God is closely bound up with a political institution—that is, the monarchy and, more specifically, the Davidic dynasty. This produced a prophetic movement that upheld moral demands and reminded the people that their identity is linked to their relationship with God, thus counterbalancing the limited perspective of the monarchy and the temptations to institutional autonomy. An excellent example of this is provided by King David's adultery with Bathsheba that was denounced by the prophet Nathan (*2 Sam* 12).

4. *The prophets and the Messiah.* The constant danger that pervaded Israel—the tribal clan which had now become a powerful kingdom—was to reduce theological thought to the material dimension and to earthly success. Thus, the fourth stage is identified by the reflections of the Major Prophets such as Isaiah, Jeremiah and Ezekiel who emphasized the greatness and universal power of the only Creator. The prophets reaffirmed the spiritual dimension of the covenant and spoke to the people of Israel of the coming of the Messiah whom Isaiah portrayed as a suffering servant.

5. *A reflection on wisdom.* The last leg of the journey, and the stage that makes direct and immediate preparations for the New Testament revelation, consists of reflection on the Wisdom of Yahweh.

After Israel's defeat and exile in Babylon, the people were left with a kingdom deprived of all its power, and this reality provided a fertile context for further reflection on and examination of Providence and the spiritual dimension of the covenant. This period gives us the books of Job, Ecclesiastes, and the Psalms. In defeat, suffering and death, the Cross is already visible in the background with its message of both sorrow and hope that will later prove to be the interpretative key for the whole of history—both of the chosen people and the entire world.

To summarize: The relationship with God and His various interventions throughout the history of the people of Israel led them to a gradual realization of the greatness of God and of his spiritual nature. Initially, He is simply recognized as the highest of all the gods because He is Creator. Yet Israel comes to see that God must be worshiped exclusively, not only because he is great but because he is unique and his ways are different from those of men. Each of these theological stages is reflected in the actual identity of Israel, an identity that is deeply and permanently characterized by a relationship with God. It was He who shaped a polytheistic clan into a united and strong people fearing neither the sun nor the moon as did the pagans. Hence, before Plato and Aristotle, and without any refined cultural tools or mechanisms, Israel had already given expression to the clearest form of monotheism ever conceived. They recognized that their identity was not defined by exterior political power, but from the spirit of being a child of God. Incidentally, the progression we have outlined not only has a historical value but is analogous to the general unfolding of the spiritual life in the individual human person.

The Attributes of God

This process of progressive spiritualization can likewise be observed in the attributes of God as He comes to meet Israel in history. The concept of the divine attributes is not a reference to some abstract and theoretical dimension. Rather, it is a response to a very practical question: How would one recognize God if one were to encounter Him? This is a question the Jews were compelled to ask throughout their history.

Firstly, if it is God who is speaking to you, He must be the stronger one—or better still, omnipotent. The perception of this specific attribute in the history of Israel is directly linked to the doctrine of creation, as is evident in the way the Book of Genesis opens. God is omnipotent and unlike other gods because He created everything out of nothing and through the sheer strength of His Word (*Ps* 33:6). He is not simply stronger than a negative principle which might act in opposition to Him, as occurs in pagan mythology. Instead, His power extends to the deepest abyss, all the way to *Sheol* (*Job* 26:5–14). Mary will recognize the Archangel Gabriel as the messenger of Yahweh, just because he said that nothing is impossible for God (*Lk* 1:37).

The omnipotence of God is bound up with the fact that God has no beginning and *has always been*. This stands in contrast to all pagan deities whose births were recounted in myths (a famous example is the birth of Venus, beautifully portrayed by Botticelli). Unlike all other nations and races, Israel did not have a theogony or account of the birth of the gods. Hence, eternity is understood in relation to the fullness of life: Yahweh is the living God, the one who simply lives (*Deut* 5:23, *Ps* 42:3). This fullness of life makes an eternal faithfulness possible, never-failing despite the waywardness of the people. Hosea was even called to marry a prostitute in order to communicate this message: God will continue to be faithful to the Elect despite their unfaithfulness to the covenant, that is, despite their idolatry.

The more Israel comes to a gradual knowledge of Yahweh, the more this spurs the people to think of His attributes in all their depth. They are urged on toward a more concrete conception of

Him, an understanding more in line with the reality of God as the source of all fulfilment. God does not *have* life; rather, He *is* Life inasmuch as He is the source of all life. Eternity is not simply understood as *always-having-been,* but as the possibility of always being present, near and effective. In this respect, eternity identifies itself with omnipresence, something fundamental for a nomadic clan and exiled people. This same reality of always being near is linked with the spiritual nature of God. Yet Israel's understanding of this attribute is often undermined by the desire to *place* God somewhere, to be able to touch Him—as in the episode of the golden calf during the exodus from Egypt (*Ex* 32).

Linked to the omnipresence of God is His omniscience—God knows all things, including the hearts and minds of all people (*Jer* 11:20, *Ps* 139:1–4). The reference to the interiority of humanity is extremely important in that the Hebrew world is not governed by deterministic necessity, as is the Greek world where everything is subject to fate. Instead, human beings, as made in the image of God, possess a will and have the capacity for love. They are endowed with an interiority, marked by freedom as opposed to necessity, an inner life the depths of which only the Creator can penetrate. Hence, if one encounters God, as happened to the Patriarchs, one can recognize Him precisely by the fact that He knows the secrets of one's heart, the sentiments that exist only within the realm of the inner conscience and are wholly inaccessible to others.

Thus, one can say that for the Israelites all of God's attributes are extremely concrete and can be traced back to the relationship God established with His people, as well as to the absolute capacity of relation by which He is characterized. Along with the entire universe, the Creator draws out of nothing the interlocutors with whom He speaks, all by means of the Word, a reality that is relational in and of itself. Eternity is the capacity always to *be present*, and never fail. In the same way, omnipresence and omniscience arise from the possibility of always having been and always remaining in relation. This relational capacity is seen as the source of all life and being.

Accordingly, the categories of Jewish thought which indicate divine activity, such as the Wisdom and the Word of Yahweh, are increasingly personified and eventually become figures of mediation. The person of God is reflected in His actions to such an extent that the relation with Him is itself personified. Here, we are dealing with a literary device that reveals a profoundly personal conception of God and, in a certain sense, prepares the way for the transition to the New Testament where Wisdom and the Word will be identified with Christ.

A relational interpretation of the attributes of God is important in order for one to understand the contrast with the philosophical and pagan world, a world governed by necessity and hence characterized by a deterministic ethos. From the Biblical perspective, God's being eternal does not mean that every event is determined by necessity. Human freedom is real just as human sin is real. Yet God is eternal in the sense that He has the absolute fullness of life, and is thereby able to deal with each and every "no" that human beings present to Him. The Creator is creative and continues to be such, for He is so great that He can even hazard the turns of human freedom. History is not predetermined. It is an authentic dialogue.

This explains how, in Israel, the perception of the divine attributes led to an ever-deepening moral dimension. The truth, inasmuch as it is a characteristic of God, is always seen in a concrete way as faithfulness, and furthermore is often accompanied in the text by goodness. Divine justice, which sometimes deals out harsh punishment, is conceived of in terms of mercy and not as necessary proportion—traditionally symbolized by scales and weights—for what God employs as a penalty is intended to distance human beings from evil. Identifying the Creator as the source of Life and every Good implies that distance from Him is bad, in the same way that distance from heat leads us to feel cold. From this perspective, it is understandable how justice and mercy are mutually referential—Yahweh is a God who loves, even with the tenderness of a mother (*Is* 49:15), and especially those who are weak and poor.

Yet, in order to understand this love, it is essential first to know God as omnipotent, otherwise the gift cannot be recognized. God does not love His people because He needs them. After all, they are a nomadic clan with nothing to offer Him. Israel is not allowed to forget this, for the relation with the Creator would be broken and the people would thereby lose their contact with the very source of life. It is precisely this omnipotence that lets us frame this relation as gift and God as love.

Throughout their history, the Israelites continued to deepen the attributes of Yahweh and spiritualized them, perceiving their intrinsic connection to the point of grasping that they are actually God Himself and so coincide with one another. To use a physical comparison, it is as if each attribute is a beam of light from the sun—to the eyes it appears white, but after passing through a prism the spectrum of light is separated into a myriad of individual colors. God is one and can be identified by each of His attributes, even though through our eyes they are separate. We distinguish omnipotence from eternity, justice from mercy, just as blues are separated from reds and greens and all the other colors within the one Light of God.

Throughout the course of their history, then, the theological thought of Israel continued to develop and, on account of their constant relationship with Yahweh, reached a singular and refined elaboration on this theme. The chosen people were being prepared to embrace, to touch, the very Word of Life, Jesus the Son of God, and this is accomplished through the constant development of a spiritual understanding of the Word of Yahweh, as well as His Omnipotence, Mercy and Wisdom.

2. The Word of the Triune God: Jesus

The God of Jesus Christ

If we look at Jesus' preaching, it is immediately evident that Yahweh is His God. Therefore, and above all, there is continuity between the Old and New Testaments. However, there is now something radically new: Jesus' *sonship*. The one who affirms this continuity is simultaneously the Son of God, Son of the same God who is One and Creator, and is Son in a manner that is humanly inconceivable in that He has the same nature as God and is one with God.

This is why the Letter to the Hebrews opens by both affirming the continuity of salvation history as well as the newness found in the Person of Christ. "Long ago, God spoke to our ancestors in many and various ways by the prophets, but in these last days he has spoken to us by a Son, whom he appointed heir of all things, through whom also he created the world" (*Hebrews* 1:1–2).

God no longer teaches solely through words and actions. Rather, He communicates *Himself*; He offers his own Son. He gives Himself. He opens up His own depths and bestows on us His Heart. This is not, then, a mere gradual, developmental understanding of the Old Testament; it is something absolutely new. It is not that in drawing nearer to God human beings have discovered that that which was previously considered to be one is in fact triune. This is something that might happen if one were looking at a single celestial body only to discover upon further examination and with the help of a more powerful telescope that it is, in fact, composed of three galaxies. Instead, God remains always and utterly one. Yet through Christ human beings have penetrated His immanence. We see Him "from the inside". Without Jesus one could never know the Trinity. Without Him, one could never know it "from within". In and through Him everything is given, such that one cannot conceive of further revelation because God has given us His very Son who is God Himself.

This explains why Jesus faithfully teaches the Law. He came not to abolish the Law but to fulfil it (*Mt* 5:17–19). The fundamental Jewish commandment, the highest affirmation of monotheism, is repeated with all of its force by Jesus himself: "Hear O Israel (*schema yisrael*), the Lord your God, the Lord is One," (*Mk* 12:29 and *Mt* 22:37). The attributes ascribed to Yahweh are also touched upon again in Jesus' teaching. In addition to being One, God is always said to be Good (*Mk* 10:18), Eternal (*Rom* 16:26), Omniscient (*Rom* 16:27), and Faithful (1 *Cor* 1:9, 2 *Th* 3:3). Yet Jesus presents these same attributes in a new, two-fold light:

These attributes assume a paternal tone.
They are also predicated of Jesus Himself, the incarnate Son.

The two are clearly related, for only in Christ, the Incarnate Son, can human beings come to know the depth of these attributes. The parable of the rich young man in Mark 10:17–22 is significant: When he calls Jesus "good teacher", he receives the answer that only God is good. What Jesus does here is present Himself as the true and proper incarnation of the divine attribute of goodness. Christ is goodness itself because he is Son and because he is one with Him who is the *source of all goodness*. Thus, Jesus is omnipotent and Lord of Life because he performs miracles such as we see in the resurrection of Lazarus (*Jn* 11:1–44); Jesus is omniscient and knows the hearts and thoughts of human beings (*Lk* 5:22, 11:7); Jesus is merciful, for he pardons sins (*Mk* 2:5–11); and Jesus is superior to the Temple (*Mt* 12:6), the Law (*Mt* 5:21), and the Sabbath (*Mt* 12:8).

The filial-paternal dimension emphasizes the attributes of mercy and love which are revealed by Christ as the meaning of the Law as a whole (*Mt* 22:34–40). We see the way in which the faithfulness of Yahweh is demonstrated in the parable of the Prodigal Son: Faithfulness is the unlimited capacity for forgiveness, a radical and relational openness that is stronger than any sin or offence (*Lk* 15:11–32). This revelation reaches its apogee in the passion and death of Christ in that moment when he is challenged by those present to come down from the Cross to which he is nailed. His accusers assure Christ that this would be the needed proof of his being the Son of God (*Mt* 27:40–43). Yet in reality, if Christ were to have come down at that moment, it would have been a demonstration of his omnipotence as merely a projection of human strength—an extension of ourselves. He would be a god of enormous strength, stronger than the nails of the Cross and those who nailed Him to it. Yet Christ wanted to reveal how the omnipotence of his Father is the omnipotence of Love. His logic is of another variety. His logic is the logic which has called the world out of nothing and is able to plunge into the nothingness of death in order to rescue human beings, bringing them out of it through the power of His self-sacrifice. The Resurrection, then, plays a fundamental role in the revelation of the one and triune God inasmuch as it confirms Jesus to be the Son of God in the sense that Jesus possesses the fullness of life within Himself. Hence, in German, as in other languages, there are two terms used to speak of Christ's returning to life: *Auferstehung* (to rise, revive, come back to life) and *Auferweckung* (to be raised). The former refers to an act of Jesus who, alone as God, rises from the grave. The latter holds a passive significance referring to the breath of life which the Father infused into the humanity of the dead Christ.

The God of Jesus Christ, therefore, embodies the same characteristics as the God of the Old Testament with the difference that
his attributes are identified one with the other and filled with infinite mercy because Yahweh is the Father and Jesus is His Son.
This deepening occurs precisely through Jesus' being identified
with these same attributes, something that arouses scandal among
the Jews. What reveals the unimaginable degree of these attributes
is what provokes the outrage, for God reveals Himself precisely by
making Himself small, in His humble descent. With his whole life,
death, and resurrection, Jesus speaks of Yahweh as being one, omnipotent, faithful, and merciful. Yet, at the same time, he demonstrates that he himself as the Son possesses these very same
attributes and thereby opens the human heart to an infinite dimension that human beings could never have come to know without Him. The very unity of God is understood and enriched in a
new way: It is no longer a unity bound up necessarily with isolation; rather, it is seen as the unity of a communion of love so complete that the Father and the Son are *one* single thing. Hence,
Yahweh is One but not alone. He is the Father and He has the
Son. Similarly, God is transcendent but does not fear to enter so
deeply into human affairs as to make Himself human. God is so
great that he can make Himself small, so high that he can bring
Himself very close, even to the point of bearing abandonment, be-
trayal, and death.

The scandal among the Jews is completely understandable.
Christ is placed on the Cross precisely because He says He is God
and claims for Himself the attributes of God, going so far as to
call Himself by the very name of Yahweh when he says, "Before
Abraham was, I am" (*Jn* 8:58). Thus, during the unjust trial in the
house of the high priest after the Last Supper, Jesus gives this answer to the question of whether He is the Christ: "I am, and you
will see the Son of Man seated at the right hand of the Power, and
coming with the clouds of heaven" (*Mk* 14:62). The reason behind

the crucifixion, then, is precisely the affirmation that this carpenter from Galilee, who had begun to preach and gather disciples, is the Son of God in a unique way since He is one with the Father. This implies the unsettling truth that God is Father and God is Son.

The Father and the Son

The affirmation of Yahweh's paternity or fatherhood is already present in the Old Testament. Just as in many pagan religions, the highest god is called "father". Yet, in Israel, this paternity was absolute for it was tied to creation. God called human beings out of nothing and created them in His image and likeness. The people experienced the care and providence of the Creator who, in turn, watched over His elect. Yahweh is the Father of the people that He created, the source of their being and identity. He is the Father of the King and Messiah (*Ps* 2:7) with whom He establishes a special relation in view of their mission. Above all, God is the Father of the poor, the widowed, and the defenceless righteous (*Ps* 103:13–14).

However, the way in which Jesus speaks of Yahweh as His Father is so entirely new and scandalous that it eventually leads to His death on the Cross. He claims God is His *Abbà* (*Mk* 14:36; *Mt* 26:53; *Lk* 22:42, 23:34, 46), a term that means *papa* in Aramaic and thereby unequivocally associates his own nature with the nature of God. This word, the simplest of words among Jewish children, solemnly reveals the divinity of Christ. Jesus can call God *papa* because He is God's Son in a unique way, essentially different from any other human being. Hence, He prays alone and always distinguishes between *my Father* and *your Father* (*Mt* 5:45, 6:1, 7:11; *Jn* 20:17), using the expression *Abbà* in circumstances of particular significance, as in the Garden of Gethsemane. The most important moments of His life are characterized precisely through this reference to the Father and to the mission received from Him. One thinks of the incident of Jesus' parents losing and then finding Him in the temple after three days, when He responds: "Did you not know that I must be in my Father's house?" (*Lk* 2:49). Or, again, at the beginning of the Paschal Mystery, when washing the disciples' feet before the Last Supper it is made clear that Jesus understood that He had received everything, i.e. every power and all the glory, from the Father, and that He had come from the Father and would return to Him (*Jn* 13:3).

The revelation of God's Fatherhood and the corresponding eternal Sonship of Jesus are found primarily in the Prologue to the Gospel of John. The Prologue is beautifully crafted out of a profound theological perspective, which, in four successive stages, presents the coming of the eternal Son to the world so as to render human beings children of God. The four stages are then retraced in the second half of the text to signify the movement of the return to the bosom of the Father (see Table 1 below). The first verse reads: "In the beginning (*arché*) was the Word (*logos*), and the Word was with God, and the Word was God" (*Jn* 1:1). This corresponds to the Book of Genesis with its affirmation that "in the beginning God created the heavens and the earth" by His word (*Gen* 1:1). In the prologue, the evangelist conveys the sense of the whole of Scripture, as though summarizing it: The novelty is that now the beginning of all that exists is not merely temporal or historical; it is, rather, the very immanence of God. From a philosophical perspective, it is extremely relevant that the evangelist uses the word *arché*, which in Greek philosophy refers to the first principle. Now this *arché* has an inner dimension, that is, an immanence, a heart—and in this immanence dwells *Logos*, a term that, like "principle" (*arché*), refers to both the *Word* of Yahweh in the Old Testament as well as the Greek philosophical *logos* as the rational foundation of all that exists.

With the affirmation that the Word-*Logos* is a person who lives in the eternity of God and who is God Himself, (a) it follows immediately that He is the origin of all created things (*Jn* 1:3) as both Light and Life (b). John the Baptist (c) spoke of Him (*Jn* 1:6–8), for in the Incarnation the true Light had to come into the world even if it was not accepted (d). In this way, we come to the heart of the Prologue where the purpose of the Incarnation is laid out: It is the realization of the sonship of those who believe in Jesus, the incarnate *Logos* who has come into the world (*Jn* 1:12–13). From this point on, it is as if the Prologue is repeating the stages announced in the first half, albeit in reverse. But the *Logos* is now explicitly identified as the Son. The Incarnation (d') is immediately spoken of again for the *Logos* became flesh and showed his glory as the only-begotten Son of the Father (*Jn* 1:14). John the Baptist is spoken of again, as well as his proclamations (c'), before the text passes on to Moses, the giver of the Law (*Jn* 1:17). In the Jewish tradition, the Law was conceived of in a way that was inseparable from creation, as the re-establishment of the original order, so much so that the Ten Commandments are called *The Ten Words*—that is, with reference to the ten words pronounced by God during the six days of creation. That is why the reference made to Moses here in the second part calls to mind the reference made to Creation (b') in John 1:3. In this symmetrical structure, which turns on the affirmation of the divine gift of sonship extended to everyone who accepts Christ, the final verse makes reference to the first part, matching the *Logos* to the only-begotten Son (a'), and creating a parallel between 'in the beginning' and 'in the bosom of the Father' (*Jn* 1:18). Thus, it is made absolutely clear that no human being could have come unaided to the reality of these truths concerning the eternal immanence of God, truths which are known to the Son alone. The content of this Gospel is thus presented as the center and meaning of the whole of human history: In the incarnate Logos, human beings discover that they have their origin in the Trinity and are likewise destined to return to the Trinity itself, as sons in the Son.

Table 1

(a) *Logos* and *arché* (*Jn* 1:1–2)		(d') The Incarnation: the *Logos* made flesh (*Jn* 1:14)
(b) Creation by means of the *Logos*, and sin (*Jn* 1:3–5)	*Center:*	(c') John the Baptist gives testimony (*Jn* 1:15)
(c) John the Baptist testifies to the Light (*Jn* 1:6–8)	Divine Sonship (*Jn* 1:11–13)	(b') The Law of Moses and the grace of the new creation (*Jn* 1:16–17)
(d) The Incarnation: the true Light in the world (*Jn* 1:9–10)		(a') The Only-Begotten Son in the bosom of the Father (*Jn* 1:18)

After the Prologue, the Gospel of John spells out in various ways the identical nature of the Father and the Son, expressed as the eternity and pre-existence of the Son. We see this in the passages, "I and the Father are one" (*Jn* 10:30); "And now, Father, glorify me in your own presence with the glory that I had with you before the world existed" (*Jn* 17:5). Everything that Jesus does is presented as a manifestation of His unique relationship with the Father.

The pre-existence of the Son is also clearly affirmed by Paul who, in *Phil* 2:5–11, carefully distinguishes between the divinity and humanity of Jesus. Inviting the Philippians to adopt the mind of Christ, he states that Jesus, though by nature divine, did not hesitate to strip himself and assume the condition of a servant, taking on human nature in obedience, even to death on the Cross, in order then to receive once more the glory of the Father and become, with his body, the Lord of all creation.

The identification of Jesus' God with Yahweh and the revelation of Jesus' eternal Sonship lead to the conclusion that God is not simply *like* a father but rather *is* Father and in an absolute way. It is not as if God were first simply a god who then at some point begins to be a father for the people or for the Messiah. Rather, through Christ, Israel discovers that God *is* Father and *has always been and always will be*, that he is Father in Himself.

The Spirit of the Father and the Son

As was mentioned in the introduction, it remains a mystery in the fullest sense of the word how the Father and the Son could be one and the same. However, this mystery certainly leads us to a *Someone,* to a Person—the Holy Spirit who is the Spirit of the Father and the Son. We are speaking here of the *Spirit of Jesus* and the *Spirit of God,* the third and most mysterious Person of the Trinity. Thomas Aquinas claimed that we lack the words to speak about Him, for He is Love, and it is always difficult to speak of Love, a mystery *par excellence.* This characteristic is in some way intrinsic to the personality of the third Person. Just as in a human being the spirit refers to what identifies him most intimately—something which is not accessible externally—so also, in God, the Spirit marks that immanent dimension and unspeakable depth which is totally beyond all capacity of comprehension. In a certain sense, He is the Light that forms the image of Christ in us, like the splendor of the gold on an icon or the glimmer that filters through the stained-glass windows of a church. He is *the* Light that shows us Jesus but does not speak of Himself in a direct way.

In the Old Testament, the term spirit, *ruah,* refers to the wind, something which is of vital importance to the rural world. Here, one is not simply speaking of a natural force but of a breath that comes from the Creator. Death is identified with the cessation of breath, and, therefore, with the loss of *ruah,* which ends up being identified as life itself. In a certain sense, the Spirit is the link between God and man inasmuch as the Spirit is God's gift that keeps man in existence. The Messiah is presented as the bearer of the fullness of the Spirit (Is 11:2) and his coming will be characterized by a unique outpouring of this Spirit according to the testimony of Acts 2:15–18 which recalls the prophecy of Joel 3:1.

The primary texts of the New Testament that refer to the third Person of the Trinity can be arranged into these three groups:

a) Passages wherein one sees the action and power of the Spirit in key moments in the life of Christ such as the Incarnation when the shadow of the Paraclete comes over Mary (*Luke* 1:35); the baptism of Jesus in the River Jordan when the Spirit descends upon Him and then guides Him in His public ministry (*Luke* 4:1); and the Resurrection, which is accomplished by the Father through the third Person (*Rom* 8:11).

b) Passages in which the Spirit sanctifies persons connected with the life of Jesus—namely, John the Baptist, Zechariah, Simeon, Elizabeth, and, above all, Mary. After these initial persons, the Paraclete proceeds to pour Himself out on to the Apostles and the members of the early Church. Hence, each and every baptized person is sanctified by the Spirit (*1 Cor* 6:11), thereby crying out *Abbà* Father in the Spirit because it is the Spirit of Christ that effects divine Sonship (*Rom* 8:15).

c) Passages wherein the Spirit is explicitly presented as a divine Person, a *Someone* distinct from the Father and the Son, for example, when he descends in the form of a dove over the Jordan (*Mt* 3:13–17, *Mk* 1:9–11, 3:21–22), and, of course, at Pentecost. He is the subject of verbs such as "to live", "to distinguish", and "to want" (*Rom* 8:11–16, *1 Cor* 3:16, *Gal* 5:17), and He guides the early Christians. He urges Philip to approach the Ethiopian eunuch (*Acts* 8:29) and Peter to go to the house of Cornelius (*Acts* 10:19–20). Above all, however, the personality of the Spirit is revealed most explicitly in the farewell discourse at the Last Supper (*Jn* 14:16–17). He is the other Comforter, fruit of the Cross, who will be sent by the Father in Jesus' name (*Jn* 14:26) and whom Christ Himself will send, the Spirit of Truth who proceeds from the Father (*Jn* 15:26).

One sees how the mission of the Spirit is completely oriented toward Christ, and is indeed inseparable from Christ. That is why he remains in the shadows as the bond of union between the Father and the Son. However, His divinity is completely affirmed, so much so that anyone who speaks a word against Him cannot be pardoned from sin, in contrast with blasphemy against Jesus (*Lk* 12:10).

The Trinity Revealed

Thus, the New Testament unequivocally presents three divine Persons who form a perfect unity in that they are the one God—Yahweh. This becomes particularly clear when the Trinity manifests itself directly at the most significant moments of Jesus' ministry.

At the beginning of Jesus' public ministry, during His baptism in the Jordan (*Mt* 3:13–17, *Mk* 1:9–11, *Lk* 3:21–22, *Jn* 1:32–34), the three Persons show themselves in their reciprocal distinction: From heaven, the Father proclaims that Jesus is His beloved Son with whom He is well pleased, and the Spirit comes down upon Him in the form of a dove. Their personal relationship is presented as a relation of love.

This episode is directly echoed in the Transfiguration, which is the immediate preparation for the Paschal Mystery (*Mt* 17:1–13, *Mk* 9:1–12, *Lk* 9:28–36). Before facing His Passion, Christ reveals Himself in His divine glory, in conversation with Moses and Elijah who represent the Law and the Prophets, and therefore reveal that what is about to take place is the meaning of Scripture as a whole. The voice of the Father repeats that Christ is the beloved Son with whom He is well pleased, telling the Apostles to listen to Him (*Mt* 17:5). Moreover, the Spirit manifests Himself in the form of a bright cloud. Christ is about to suffer and be stripped of everything to the point of death and, as at the beginning of His public ministry, he is presented in the light of the Father's love.

The baptism in the Jordan, with the immersion in and emergence from the water, is an image of death and resurrection to new

25

life, and becomes reality in an unimaginable way in the Paschal Mystery with the baptism of the Cross followed by the Resurrection after three days in the tomb. The words of Christ that conclude Matthew's Gospel find their origin in this very mystery in that the Risen One, through his missionary mandate, sends his disciples into the whole world so that every person might be baptized *in the name of the Father and of the Son and of the Holy Spirit* (*Mt* 28:19). The fullness of the Life of Christ must be communicated to all by way of the apostolate and incorporation in the Church through baptism. The fact that Jesus explicitly cites the three Persons, claiming at the same time that they constitute one name in the singular, has become the foundation of both the liturgical practices of the Church as well as of every theological treatment of the Trinity. The three divine Persons must be one and the same, yet, in an irreducible way, are three distinct *subjects* with proper names and proper characteristics. One God in three Persons: Father, Son and their Spirit.

Christianity is thus identified with the communication and the flowing out into history of the life of Christ—namely, Trinitarian life. This life, which flows out of the bosom of the Father, conquers death. This is why Paul emphasizes how all things in Christian existence are marked by the Trinity: The concept of vocation is presented with reference to the three divine Persons as its starting point (*2 Thes* 2:13–14), and the same is true for the multitude of charisms, ministries and ecclesial functions (*1 Cor* 12:4–6), and hence the unity of the Church itself (*Eph* 4:4–6). Some of these formulas have been passed on into the liturgy: "The grace of the Lord Jesus Christ and the love of God and the communion of the Holy Spirit be with you all" (*2 Cor* 13:14).

It is in Christ, then, that human beings have come to know the immanence of God—that is, his being in and of himself Father, Son and Holy Spirit. God is not what we imagine him to be if we depart from our expectations. He is *one* as we think, but he is *one* in a way that passes beyond all human expectation. His unity is simultaneously that of Being and that of Love, of a Love that is Being and Being that is Love. This explains why the Christian God can be known in his immanence only when one surrenders oneself to the wonder of God's *being one and triune*—not *being one notwithstanding the fact of being three*, but rather one *precisely because* triune. That is, he is triune because of the mystery of the love between the Father, the Son and the Holy Spirit. Beginning with Christ's teachings, this spectacular revelation has enriched human thought, starting with the initial formulations of the Church Fathers and continuing along the centuries through an increasing immersion in this very Mystery of Love.

3. The Response to the Word:
The Faith of the Church

Sources of Thought

In the light of all that has been explained in the two previous chapters, one can understand how Christianity is not simply a moral or philosophical doctrine but is identified with the very Person of Christ. Revelation is not a collection of theories but is a Man who is at the same time God, the eternal Son of the Father. In the life, death and resurrection of Jesus, we see that it is impossible to reduce the mystery of the one and triune God to some observable reality already present in nature or history. The scandal of the Paschal Mystery cannot be eliminated, nor is there any room for shortcuts or simplifications. Human thought is called to continuous development, ever expanding its depths without ever exhausting revealed reality— and this revealed reality is Christ Himself with His Trinitarian life.

As Peter's discourse in Acts 2:22–36 shows, the first moment of the evangelical announcement presents Christ and the Trinity together to affirm the reality of the salvation offered to every human being: true life is now accessible, because Jesus is true God, and this means that God is Father, Son and Holy Spirit.

Thus, the entirety of Christian life, beginning with baptism, is marked by the presence of the Trinity. According to the evidence of the *Didaché* at the end of the first century, this sacrament was performed by way of three-fold immersion or three effusions of water, accompanied by the invocation of the three divine Persons in obedience to Christ's missionary mandate (*Mt* 28:19). The Profession of faith, or the Creed, was linked to baptism and was the basis of the preparation of the catechumens. From the very beginning, the Creed has had a three-part structure, with an article for each of the three divine Persons that corresponds to the three-fold question, "Do you believe in the Father? Do you believe in the Son? Do you believe in the Holy Spirit?" These questions were subsequently condensed into a single text. Brief formulations of faith were already present in the New Testament (see *Acts* 8:37; *Eph* 1:13; *1 Tim* 6:12; *Heb* 4:14), such as the very simple and basic expression "Jesus is the Lord" of *Romans* 10:9. The force behind this profession is particularly evident in the Acts of the Martyrs. In the moment of accepting the penalty of death, the martyrs make the choice for a true life that no one can take from them—the life of Christ, eternal Son of the Father.

Trinitarian references permeate the whole of Christian liturgy, especially the celebration of the Eucharist (see Hippolytus of Rome, *Apostolic Tradition,* 4) and Christian prayer, which like Jewish prayer begins and ends by invoking the name of God. Yet Christian prayer distinguishes itself from Jewish prayer precisely when, in confessing God to be one, it claims that He is triune. One thinks, for example, of the sign of the cross that usually begins and ends the act of praying. In fact, Christian prayer is always addressed *to* the Father, *through* the Son, *in* the Holy Spirit.

Baptism, the creeds, the liturgy, prayer and the profession of faith of the martyrs are all primary sources of Trinitarian reflection. All the life of the early Church is founded on the Trinity and the divinity of Christ. This life is like a unique fountain from which springs an unprecedented body of thought that gradually grows in clarity until it shines forth in Christian dogma.

The Early Church Fathers and the Theology of the Logos

Those who first attempted to formulate this idea and continue to develop it were the Fathers of the Church. The role they played was authentically paternal. For human beings, the father is crucial in the exploration of reality. While the mother gives birth to and nurtures the child, constituting the origin and material dimension, it is the father who represents the world once the child comes out of the mother's womb. It is the father who brings the child out of the home and reveals the external dimension. In this role, the capacity to help develop thought concerning new things is fundamental—it is not going where one has already been, where a person was born, but interacting with what he or she has never encountered before, developing new categories.

The Fathers of the Church carried out an analogous role with respect to revelation, and their writings are normative in Christian thought—they constitute the first response to the Word of God who enters into history. As Joseph Ratzinger wrote, "to understand the Word one must enter into dialogue with those who first heard, responded, and considered these things. Even though these early attempts are marked by limitation, only through these can one gain access to the sense of the revealed newness, precisely because their response signifies the sense of the Word that was addressed to them in the first place."[3] To give an example, it is like one single term having two different meanings in two different languages—in English, the term *gift* has the same root as the German word *Gift*, which means venom. It is essential to know what language a particular people speak in order to understand what is meant by a particular term used by someone.

The early Christian thinkers had their own cultural baggage

---

3   J. Ratzinger, *Principles of Catholic Theology* (San Francisco: Ignatius Press, 1987), 148–152.

inherited from the cultural and philosophical education of their time. These tools were put to the service of understanding and communicating the newness that had been revealed. As can also be seen in the New Testament writings, there were various cultural components in play. In particular, the Semitic and Hellenistic elements emerge, the latter being dominant throughout the Mediterranean regions at that time. The different categories were reworked and adapted to express the new message.

The writers of the first two centuries, like Ignatius of Antioch and Clement of Rome, do not offer what might be called speculative development as such. Rather, they write letters in the Pauline style, reasserting the doctrinal nucleus of the oneness of God and the divinity of Christ. Their teachings directly echo the teachings of the Apostles, of whom some of them were disciples, such as Polycarp of Smyrna who received his instruction directly from the Apostle John. There is often a strong nostalgia for the humanity of the Lord reflected in their works, with the corresponding affirmation of the reality of his flesh.

It is in the Apostolic Fathers of the second century that we witness the makings of a first nucleus of doctrine, generally as a response to the attacks launched against the Church by the Jews or the gentile pagans. Confronted with these persecutions, these early Christian thinkers wrote Apologies, or treatises of defense, like the one written by Aristides addressed to the emperor Antoninus. These writings present arguments of a philosophical nature which share many of their presuppositions with those of their interlocutors, such as a demonstration of God's unity by looking at the presence of movement, beauty and order within the world.

Among the Apologetic Fathers, the most important is Justin Martyr who was born in Palestine and martyred in Rome in 165 A.D. He was a philosopher by profession and founded his Christian thought on a synthesis of the ontological depth of Platonism and the positive vision of the Stoic conception of matter. Justin's approach is paradigmatic in that he freely takes recourse in an eclectic way in different philosophical languages shared at that time, correcting the shortcomings of one compared with Christian doctrine with the advantages of another, and vice versa. After his conversion, he established a philosophical-theological school in Rome.

His doctrine pivots on the *Logos,* a term that, beginning with John's Prologue, had acquired new value and thereby becomes essential to the development of Christian doctrine. In Greek, it had the meaning of thought, word and reason. Now, it is the eternal Son of the Father. Justin Martyr sees in the *Logos* itself an element of connection between Greek philosophy and the new reality that has been revealed. Through the second Person of the Trinity, the history of man and the search for truth of any age can now be placed in continuity. Whoever has discovered anything true has come to know the *Logos,* albeit in a partial form. The rational structure of creation is, in fact, identical for all human beings and finds its origin in God himself—that is, in the Son through whom everything that exists has been made (*Jn* 1:3). This is why Socrates and Heraclites might be called Christian (Justin Martyr, *I Apologia,* 46. 2.1–3.6), and likewise any element of truth can be called Christian regardless of where it is found. The *Logos* itself is presented as the bridge to the Old Testament, for the manifestations of God in the history of Israel like the burning bush on Mount Horeb (*Ex* 3:14) are attributed to the *Logos.*

The *Logos* fulfils the function of mediation and unification. This may, however, lead to misunderstanding in that it may seem that the existence of the *Logos* is necessarily connected to history and creation. Instead, the *Logos* is the thought of God that is divine and eternal yet turned toward the world, like the Wisdom of Yahweh in which everything has been thought, His plan of which *Sirach* 1:1–11 speaks, for example. This moves Justin Martyr to call only the Father God and renders him incapable of expressing in his thought the perfect equality among the divine Persons. The problem lies on the level of formulation and the language employed: Faith in the divinity of Christ is not in doubt, but the conceptual instruments available have yet to be refined. One must keep in mind that Greek philosophy affirmed the existence of a continual ascent of ontological steps that connected the world to its first principle. One might think of the Unmoved Mover in the metaphysical doctrine of Aristotle. From this perspective and inherited vision, the *Logos* is seen as an intermediate figure.

Creation, instead, requires the introduction of a radical discontinuity between God and the world. The design with which God creates all things, though existing totally within God, is the origin of what God establishes outside of Himself, as in the case of a painter who conceives his or her work. This design, identified with the *Logos,* runs the risk of being stuck somewhere halfway between God and the world as a mediator, because the existence of the idea of an artistic production is necessarily linked with the artwork itself. Justin Martyr is unable to free the Son from all connection with creation, something that is perceived as a cause of inferiority. Precisely because the *Logos* exists in relation, it seems bound to the world through relation itself and not able to be called God like the Father. Justin's thought is still too much tied to a pagan philosophical concept that holds relation to be something of a bond or necessary tie. The relationship between God and his action needs further development. There is still a need to distinguish the role of the Son within the Trinity—perfect God and one in being with the Father—from His role of mediation carried out as a result of the Incarnation through which He became perfect Man. The Christ, in fact, is not an intermediate ontological level, midway between God and the world. He is utterly and completely eternal and divine as the Son of the Father, and true man inasmuch as He is the Incarnate Son, born of Mary in time and space.

Irenaeus and Gnosticism

Irenaeus pursued a different path of reflection and succeeded in recognizing the unity of history without subordinating the Son. Born in Smyrna sometime between 140–160, he knew Polycarp, a disciple of the Apostle John. The imprint of the Prologue to the Fourth Gospel is clearly present in his theology.

His principal work, *Against Heresies*, is very much a bastion of defence against Gnosticism, something that might be considered a heresy although it is better understood as an attitude, a constant temptation of the human spirit. Gnosticism's obscure origins begin in the Persian world, and its distinctive characteristic is the belief that human beings can save themselves by accessing a hidden knowledge reserved solely for the elect few. The conceptual foundation for this possibility consists in a dualistic vision of the world that distinguishes a good and a bad principle, together with a hierarchical conception of ontology. As in Greek thought, the Gnostics likewise believed that the world is founded on a scale of various metaphysical levels that unite it with the First Principle. This scale, or staircase, constitutes a progressive decline—the various intermediary levels are derived from an original unity through necessary emanation, that is, through a partial, and thereby corrupting, emission. Matter and diversity are subsequently understood to be intrinsically evil because they are considered the results of decay or decline. The Gnostic sought the opportunity to ascend to a purely spiritual dimension, the dimension of the First Principle, through knowledge of the sequence of emanations. Depending on the particular Gnostic school, these could number as many as thirty.

Gnosticism was notably attractive for the ease with which it explained evil and provided the individual with the possibility of saving himself on his own. Hence, it gained momentum even in the Christian world. Irenaeus, Bishop of Lyons, was concerned by the infiltration of Gnosticism and constructed a doctrine founded upon the unity of God and the unity of history. The goodness of the world is rooted in the freedom of the Creator who created everything out of nothing solely out of love. All things find their origin in the Trinity and all things move toward the Trinity; and so all things are born of freedom and move toward freedom. Hence, the necessary connection between the beginning and the end, or between the efficient and final cause that characterized the classical philosophical vision, is superseded. Since the Father, the Son and the Holy Spirit are one God, the fruit of their action must be entirely marked by their characteristics: There is no ontological ladder that determines a growing negativity when one distances oneself from the summit. Everything that rises from divine action is directly marked by the unity and goodness of God. Divine being and acting are directly linked, so much so that the Son and the Holy Spirit are represented as the hands of the Father.[4] The whole of history is perceived to be within the firm embrace of the Trinity.

The notion that man is truly saved from death through Christ is the basis of Irenaeus' thought, for man has received His life from Christ, He who is eternal life, the very life of God. If Christ is not perfect God, but a mere intermediary—as the philosophical notion of the *Logos* might lead one to believe—then salvation is not real. Unlike the philosopher Justin, Irenaeus was a bishop and his primary concern was therefore to defend the faithful in his care from the dangers posed by Gnosticism. For this reason he is less speculative. Instead, he takes a more stable and certain route and opposes the *conception of derivation,* or the Gnostic position of hierarchical ontology, with unity. He states with considerable force that the *Logos* is the thought of the Father, eternal and immanent to Him, without implying any dependence in creative action since creation is a purely free act. The action of God is a pure gift and is not

4   Irenaeus, *Demonstration of the apostolic preaching,* 5.

marked by necessity, precisely because the very being of God is characterized by the gift of authentic Sonship. Unity resides in the gift, and the gift bears unity when approached from a perspective akin to that of John's Gospel. Irenaeus' theological thought is indicative of a future line of development that will be taken up later and perfected by Athanasius and the Cappadocians who were equipped with new conceptual instruments.

Tertullian and Modalism

Tertullian, who lived into the first decades of the third century, made the first great contribution to the elaboration of Trinitarian thought in the Latin world. He composed brilliant formulations that would unmistakably influence all subsequent theology. He was the first, for example, to apply the term *Trinity* (in Latin *Trinitas*) to God.

Tertullian was faced with the Modalist heresy. This is a version of Monarchianism, which claimed that only the Father is God. This heresy reduced the Trinity to the first Person as a singular principle which, in Greek, is precisely "monarchy" (*monos* + *arché*), as is understood analogously in the political rendering of the term.

The first versions of this heresy emerge among the adoptionists, who were already present in the East as early as the second century and, at times, were linked with Semitic circles. They considered Christ to be a mere man, adopted by the Father at the moment of his baptism in the Jordan or through the Resurrection, and thereby endowed with inhuman powers that transformed him into some kind of superman. The most notorious of these adoptionists was Paul of Samosata, Bishop of Antioch from 260 to 280. According to his idea of things, God was not Father *in and of Himself,* but only with respect to a human being he had adopted. The Son is entirely reduced to the dimension of God's action, which is the same as excluding him from the divine Being.

Tertullian was confronted with a more evolved version of Monarchianism, known as Modalism, a current with origins in the East though it was significantly developed in the West. The three Persons are seen as masks that the one God wears interchangeably according to the nature of his presence in history. Noetus, Bishop of Smyrna, was largely responsible for this notion. In 180, he began to preach that the Son is in reality the Father, and in such a way that it was the Father Himself who suffered on the Cross. In 213, Tertullian refuted Praxeas, who had further extended Noetus' notion to the Holy Spirit, as Sabellius would also do some years later. The latter was a Libyan priest who, after moving to Rome, spread a systematized form of this heresy: The Father is the mask of God in the Old Testament, the Son is the mask of God in the New, and the Holy Spirit is the mask that God assumed after Pentecost.

In this version of Monarchianism, too, the Trinity is understood only on the level of God's *action* and not on that of his *being*. This was facilitated by the fact that, at the time, no true concept of person existed in the way we understand it today after centuries of Christian culture. The Greek term to which these heretical thinkers had recourse was *prosopon*, which literally means *character*, like the *character* in a theatrical play. Precisely for this reason, the same term also took on the meaning of *mask*. To conceive of God as three *prosopa* meant understanding Him as three different modes, three aspects of a single reality.

Tertullian responds by strengthening the concept of *Person* as much as he can through the theoretical tools available to him. Thus, he makes use of the corresponding Latin term which has a concrete juridical value as a legal subject. The Father, the Son and the Holy Spirit are title-holders of the right to ownership of the one substance. Thus, the Trinity is defined as *una substantia, tres personae*, according to a distinction of order but not substance, power or dignity.[5] This

5   *Adversus Praxean,* 2.

formula was to become normative in the development of Latin Trinitarian thought. Tertullian associates it with other particularly effective expressions, such as "the Trinity of one, single Divinity, Father, Son and Holy Spirit."[6]

Yet Tertullian's theology is, again, still marked by the limitations of his time—he distinguishes the Father and the Son through recourse to an analogy of matter, claiming that the latter is a portion (*portio*) of the former.[7] Divine unity is thereby conceived of as analogous in many ways to an organism, something that has vital connections within itself. Hence, even though he affirms that the Father has never been without the Son, nevertheless, in some of his texts Tertullian seems to imply the Son's dependence on creation, falling into the same limitations of expression as previously read in Justin.

Clement and Origen: A Christian Culture

Through what has been presented thus far, we can see how necessary and difficult it was to develop authentic Christian thought. Revelation had introduced something so radically new that no language existed to express it properly. A single brilliant mind was not enough—a series of lives were needed, devoted in their commitment to a continual, deeper understanding of the Mystery.

Thus, the Church Fathers edged forward, little by little, both in coining new words as well as altering the meanings of ancient terminology, and so a true Christian culture began to slowly bloom. Christian culture was also marked by a great openness to what human beings had already discovered through their own inquiry, as well as by a strong awareness of their own human identity as based on the relation to the God Who is one and triune.

6   *De pudicitia,* 21.
7   *Adversus Praxean,* 9.

Alexandria played a key role in this movement. Founded in the year 331 by Alexander the Great, this Egyptian city became the important epicentre of commercial and cultural activity in the Mediterranean during the Hellenistic Age. It is traditionally held that the *Septuagint*, the Greek version of the Bible, was edited here within a climate of interaction and dialogue between the Semitic world and classical culture.

The third century brought the development of proper theological schools, both in Alexandria and Antioch. The former city was characterized by its famed attention to the interpretation of sacred texts, through the use of sophisticated philological and hermeneutical tools, and to rational criticism which had recourse to the various conclusions of contemporary philosophy. The biblical exegesis here was rather allegorical, whereas in Antioch the more literal interpretation prevailed. The two schools provided contrasting—though both legitimate—approaches to understanding the meaning of Scripture. These approaches corresponded to the two different perspectives regarding the mystery of Christ that can be traced back to the difference between the Synoptic Gospels and the Gospel of John.

In the Synoptic Gospels, in fact, we witness the chronological process of the Apostles' discovery that the man whom they met and followed was God, whereas the Gospel of John, the last of the four to be written, begins, in the very Prologue, from the divinity of the Word and from there moves to His Incarnation.

In Alexandria, there was a tendency to think of revelation beginning with the divine *Logos* and His being made flesh, as read in *John* 1:14. This is why theologians in Alexandria emphasized the divinity of Christ, running the risk of leaving His humanity in the shadows as if the assumed flesh were incomplete humanity and His nature were only divine. Yet in Antioch there was greater emphasis on the humanity of Christ, which ran the risk of dividing His unity, as if the divine *Logos* were united to a complete man who had already been formed. The Christ is one, single divine Person in two natures—both human and divine. Alexandria risked reducing Him to one Person with one nature, whereas Antioch favored acknowledging two Persons and two natures.

It is no wonder, then, that the Alexandrian school greatly developed the theology of the *Logos,* attempting, as Justin had done, to regain for Christian reflection all the truths discovered by Greek philosophy.

Clement, who died in the second decade of the second century, was one of the figureheads of this school of thought. He fervently claimed that the existence of God is a truth that one can come to know through reason alone, and he speaks of man as a religious creature who is endowed with a certain instinct toward God (*Stomata* 4, 14). At the same time, however, he emphasizes that the Trinitarian dimension is beyond the grasp of this instinct and is only accessible through revelation.

Clement ardently opposed the heresy of Marcion, which distinguished the evil God of the Old Testament from the merciful God of the New Testament, thereby separating creation and redemption. Clement based his argument on the oneness of God, founded in His infinite being. For there simply cannot be two infinites.[8]

Clement's legacy was subsequently taken up by Origen, one of the greatest human minds in history. Born in Alexandria around the year 185, Origen was the son of a martyr. He himself died from the wounds of torture endured for love of the faith in 253. With powerful exegetical ability, vast erudition and exceptional linguistic competence, he compiled a *corpus* of doctrine that stands as a magnificent display of theology and the study of the meaning of the whole of Scripture, essentially showing how Christian doctrine consists of the thought pertaining to the history of salvation.

8   *Protrepticus,* 6.

Origen demonstrated how all the different divine attributes are united in the single attribute of the Good in such a way that Being and Goodness are identified with each other (*On John*, 2:7). Everything that exists and everything that God has done for us is rooted in Love. Love is the cause of everything, whereas evil does not have divine cause but instead originates in human freedom (*Against Celsus* 6:55). The omnipotence of God does not mean that He can commit evil, for it is repugnant to His divinity and His being—just as that which is sweet by nature cannot produce something that is bitter (*Against Celsus, 3*:70). To understand Scripture one needs to remember that God is purely spiritual and that the corporeal images and ways man speaks about Him as if He were a man, as are common in the Old Testament, serve only to help human beings understand the message by adapting it to human ways of speaking.

Everything in Origen's thought aims at highlighting the role of freedom in the action of both God and man. For example, the eternity and omniscience of God does not mean that human beings are compelled to carry out what He has decided in the beginning. God does not exist within time, and His eternity is not a mere backward or forward unlimited extension of the temporal dimension, like a finite segment that becomes an endless straight line and belongs to the same geometrical dimension. If it were so, human beings would be predetermined by God's will before their births, being no more than puppets, as Plato famously remarks (*Laws* 644d–645b). Our existence would be fixed in advance and we would be left with nothing but the choice to accept or reject some preordained plan. This is not the Christian vision of reality, but rather that of pagans and fatalism, even though today it unfortunately does carries some weight. An example of this would be the claim that love between two people is only possible between those who are like two halves of the same apple—predetermined and compatible. If this were true, there would be no such thing as human love. Any vocation, whether or not specifically for marriage, would be pure and simple predetermination and not the fruit of an authentic and free dialogue.

For this reason, in his exchange with the pagan Celsus, Origen explains that prophecies did not come to pass because they were prophesied. Rather, they were made because they were going to come to pass (*Against Celsus*, 20, 2). The causal arrow can move backwards through time because the eternity of God is contemporary in every age. Thus, through his relation with God, the prophet can know what will come to pass, on a temporal line that runs into the future.

Origen sets himself against the Modalists in the Eastern world, underscoring the personality of the Father, Son and Holy Spirit. He is the first to call the latter the *Trias*, the Greek equivalent for Trinity (*On John*, 10:39 and 6:33). He also opposes the Gnostics in developing the theology of the generation of the Son: In appealing to the spirituality of God, he claims that it is not a matter of emanation or material separation, but that, in God, generation is a purely spiritual act and, therefore, eternal (*On First Principles*, 1,2,4:6). Hence the Father has never been alone without the Son. As far as terminology goes, however, Origen's intensive use of the theology of the *Logos* gives rise to some expressions that would cause confusion and equivocation in the following century. These will be understood in a subordinationist sense, that is, as a claim of the ontological inferiority of the Son with respect to the Father. Origen says, for example, that the *Logos* is *deuteros Theos*, or God of a second category (*Against Celsus*, 5:39) and God through participation, whereas only the Father is true God (*On John*, 2:2). Thus, the influence of the philosophical tools of Neoplatonism push him to consider the *Logos*—and not the Christ, or the Incarnate *Logos*—as mediator between the Father and the world. Here, the second Person has yet again an intrinsic relation to creation.

Notwithstanding Origen's enormous deepening of doctrine,

one sees the limitations that were likewise present in Justin's work. The content of faith is Christian, but the expressive language is still inadequate inasmuch as the proper conceptual instruments have yet to come into existence. As is also evident in his anthropology, which strongly approximates human beings to angels, what is lacking is a theology of natures that articulates the relation between God and the world more effectively. This new conceptual instrument emerges only in the fourth century through the efforts to clarify doctrine during the storm of the Arian crisis.

Nicaea and Arianism

We now find ourselves in a significantly altered historical climate. In 313, Emperor Constantine converted to Christianity and nearly three hundred years of Christian persecution came to a definitive end. Theological debates now moved to the fore and assumed public and political importance. It was now possible to meet not only in local synods, as many had already been doing, but as full ecumenical councils bringing together bishops and representatives of the entire Church.

Arius was a presbyter of Alexandria who was ordained in his early fifties with an already troubled past, having been excommunicated and readmitted into the Church before his ordination. He was the parish priest of a church in the port and a respected preacher. Yet his statements disturbed some of the faithful because he claimed that the Son had been created in time and that he was simply the first among creation. They took this to the Bishop of Alexandria, who, after a discussion with Arius before the clergy of the diocese, convened a local synod to excommunicate him. The heresy spread rapidly for various reasons. There was an attractiveness in its way of simplifying the mystery. Moreover, Arius had many contacts among the bishops, particularly in the East, where the heresy was also welcomed for reasons of episcopal rivalry. Yet, the main reason for this heresy's taking hold was because it furnished an answer to a question that had hitherto been left untouched on account of the lack of adequate conceptual instruments. The expressive limits of the theology of the *Logos*, a theology that reached its apex in Origen's work and yet was only partially covered by him, had side-effects that could not be overlooked. The still inadequate form was in danger of undermining and obscuring the content. It was imperative that the tension between the claim that the Father has never been without the Son and the definition of the Son as God through participation be resolved. To have being through participation necessarily requires a created state. Was the *Logos* on the side of God or on the side of the created, or was he in some intermediate sphere? The doctrine of creation seems to exclude this third possibility, yet, at the same time, the connection of the *Logos* with creation itself—as the very thought of the Creator—seems to demand precisely this. Arius cleanly resolved the question by placing the *Logos* in creation.

At this point, Constantine decided to convene an ecumenical council to restore religious peace. The central point of the issue in question was, precisely, the Sonship of Christ. This implies that the second Person of the Trinity is generated, but, according to the common claim of theologians and philosophers, God cannot have an origin in something external. The Second Person must thereby be *ungenerated* because he is eternal. The simple solution advanced by Arius is that, precisely because he is generated, the Son is God but only of a second category. At a certain point, the Son came to be associated with the divinity of the Father through an act of grace but is not eternal by nature. So, if the Son is not eternal by nature, neither can the Father be 'Father' from eternity, and hence God would be God prior to being Father.

An answer finally emerges through a purification of human language that in itself cannot fully express the Mystery, but which comes to create new words and concepts to express the radical novelty of revelation and avoid misrepresenting it. Thus, in the first place, a distinction was made between *ungenerated being* in the sense of being eternal, something common to the Father and the Son, and *ungenerated being* inasmuch as one is Father of the Son. The first meaning refers to substance—that is, to what the Persons of the Trinity are together. The second meaning refers to their being as individual Persons and to their reciprocal relationships.

The point here, then, is that the claim of the New Testament that Christ is the eternal Son of the Father reveals to man for the first time a *generated being* who is not temporal and is not marked by the limits of corporeity—an eternal *generated being*. This is something radically new because it is not found in nature. Correspondingly, it implies a new concept of Fatherhood, understood in the sense of pure gift of self and relation to the Son. It is on account of the doctrine of Nicaea that we understand that the Father is and always has been Father precisely because He has always had a Son in such a way that without the Son the Father cannot be Himself.

However, in order to understand this step, one needs to be able to distinguish in the Gospels between what Christ accomplished as God—the resurrection of Lazarus, the restoration of sight to the man born blind, or his own resurrection—and what Christ did in his humanity—being hungry, crying or even dying. The different Gospel narratives have to be attributed, respectively, to one of the two natures of Christ. Arius and his followers used passages relating to the humanity of Christ as proof of his inferiority to the Father. In particular, the supreme difficulty was found in the obedience of the Son, on the basis of the principle that to obey is a sign of inferiority.

The headcount at the Council was somewhere between 250 and 300 bishops of whom only four were from the West. However, among the latter was Hosius of Cordoba who was most likely the papal legate because he is always named first in official documents.

Bishop Alexander was accompanied by his deacon Athanasius who later succeeded him and was eventually to play a role of great importance in theological disputes. After the initial sessions, the assembly adopted the creed of the church of Caesarea, with some modifications to eliminate all interpretative ambiguity. The sessions were long and reached a conclusion only on account of the intervention of Constantine, who after making a series of threats exiled two Bishops unwilling to sign the accord. This use of force caused considerable trouble in the wake of the council because it left insufficient time to come to a true agreement or to elaborate a common language.

The Creed is substantially the one we still recite today, with only a few modifications made at the Council of Constantinople in 381. It is characterized by the following elements:

1. The term *Son of God* can be understood only in the sense of being *of the same substance as the Father;* He is light from light, just as He is true God from true God.
2. He is, therefore, *Begotten, not made,* and so is not created, but eternal.
3. That is to say, He is *consubstantial with the Father.*

In Greek, this last adjective is *homousios,* or "of the same substance". It has been particularly criticized in the course of history as a term that has its origin solely in philosophy. It was a cause of concern that the language of philosophy replaced the language of theology. Yet, it was precisely the need to understand the meaning of Scripture—together with the necessary task of sharing this with all men and all generations—that demanded this happen. There was never a question of rejecting philosophy. In fact, it is impossible to elaborate theology without it. The question, instead, concerned the appropriate modifications to philosophical language so as to express the radical newness of revelation while avoiding those limitations that would obscure the irreducible newness of Christianity.

On account of the sudden interruption of the working session, together with the complexity of the question, the years that followed Nicaea were marked by bitter struggles, and these can be summarized in the following three phases:

1. The *first phase*. From Nicaea up until the death of Constantine in 337 with the rehabilitation of Arius and the *volte-face* (turncoats) of many who had accepted the Creed.

2. The *second phase*. From 337 to 361, during the time of the Emperors Constantius and Constans. These are the years when Arianism triumphed on account of imperial protection. The heresy was actually used by Constans as a means of uniting the empire. More and more bishops faithful to Nicaea were exiled, among them Pope Liberius.

3. The *third phase*. From 361 to 380. In 361, the Emperor Julian, called the Apostate because he abjured the Christian faith and tried to restore paganism, gave freedom back to the Church and the orthodox bishops, and they returned to their respective churches. The Arians themselves began to break into groups—there were those who maintained that the Son is totally *unlike* the Father, and those who claimed that the Son is *of similar substance* though not identical in substance with the Father.

Athanasius and the Theology of the Natures

The resulting confusion after the Council of Nicaea brought to light the fact that a single term was not enough to eliminate all possible ambiguities and equivocation. *Homousios* could be understood in three ways:

1. The Son is only like the Father;
2. He is of the same substance as the Father in a specific sense, like two men that belong to the same human species;
3. Or else, it might represent a numerical unity, that is, that the entire singular substance would belong to both of them.

Decisive progress was needed in the theological argumentation. This progress finally arrived with Athanasius, an impressive theologian and pastor who died in 373 after enduring exile on five different occasions. There are two cardinal aspects to his doctrine––namely, the use of soteriological argumentation and the introduction of a new conceptual instrument with his theology of nature. These two elements are, in a certain sense, interwoven with each other. The entire foundation of Athanasius' thought is the notion that, if the *Logos* is not eternally God, then we have not actually been saved. If He who became incarnate has not communicated the life of the Father, which He has in its fullness, then man has not been made divine.

As can be seen, this debate did not hinge on merely theoretical questions—what was at stake was the very essence of the gospels. Yet, in order for the *Logos* to be understood as eternal and true God, there was still the need to overcome the philosophical conception that bound the *Logos* to creation as a thought of the Creator, the Father. Athanasius accomplished this with his theology of the natures. In fact, he actually begins by claiming the distinction between God and the world in terms of differences in nature, identifying the Father, Son and Holy Spirit with one single nature, both eternal and uncreated (*Against the Arians,* 1, 18). There exists but one, single, infinite nature with these attributes, whereas all other existing natures are creatures, finite and with a beginning in time. The distance between these and the Creator is infinite. Thus, the *Logos* can no longer remain halfway between God and the world but is fully inserted in the immanence of God.

As is clear, the debate revolves around the divine attributes, and these must be understood in a theological manner. Arius claims that God is eternal and immutable, and therefore the Son, being generated, cannot be God. Athanasius responds by distinguishing human generation (where a father precedes his son temporally) from eternal generation in the Trinity (*Against the Arians,* 1:14). In the Trinity, everything is eternal, and immutability itself is invoked against the Arian lines of reasoning: If God were to have at some point begun to be Father, as the Arians maintained, then God would have undergone a change. The divine attributes move from being conceived of in a merely philosophical manner—beginning with the creaturely experience of man—to a new dimension rendered accessible by revelation in which these attributes are understood in a more perfect way. Openness to the faith is, then, never opposition to reason, rather the way in which reason is led to unfold and develop more perfectly.

Yet this requires moving toward a form of thought that gives new value to the idea of relation. For the Father cannot be Himself without the Son, in that thinking of one is to think immediately of the other because they are a single reality, one thing. Father, Son and Holy Spirit are a single nature and a single, eternal substance, uncreated and immutable precisely in their reciprocal references to each other: As the Son is the image of the Father, so the Spirit is the image of the Son (*Letter to Serapion,* IV, 3.3). This development is fundamental because the First Principle, the very source of being, is identified as a Person and not an abstract reality—everything comes from Someone who is also the source of all goodness. Thus, the biblical message is more and more understood by opening thought to a conception of Fatherhood that was previously unimaginable and which now exceeds all human expectations.

Yet Athanasius still does not succeed in fully distinguishing the generation of the Son from the procession of the Holy Spirit, for he says that the latter, too, is an image as the Son is an image. Hence, Athanasius leaves a vulnerable spot open to the Tropici, a heretical group who deny the divinity of the Holy Spirit, as we shall see in the last part of the chapter. Nor can Athanasius develop the personal characteristics of each divine Person in a full and complete way because he still lacks the means to do so. For example, he cannot employ a specific term to indicate the divine *Person* insofar as the expressions *substance* (*ousia*) and *hypostasis* are still synonymous in his mind, as they were in Greek at the time. The latter term indicates substance in its concrete existence, but not exactly what we mean today when we say *person*. The perception of a personal dimension, with its inalienable value, specifically emerges in the reflection on the Trinitarian revelation and did not exist in cultures prior to Christianity. Nevertheless, the progress made by Athanasius was enormous, and the two main pillars of his thought prove to be very fruitful in the subsequent work undertaken by the Cappadocian Fathers.

The Cappadocian Fathers and Relation

Basil (†378), his brother, Gregory of Nyssa († 396), and his friend, Gregory Nazianzus (†390), make a singular mark on the history of Christian thought. Each has his own style and character, each is quite different, something that is also witnessed in the discussions carried out among the three of them. Yet the work they produced together is endowed with a sense of deep communion that is the result of great faith and a humble trust in the possibility of thought. The three of them are at once impressive theologians and true mystics. They formed a kind of society for theological progress. Basil, the figurehead and capable organizer, developed the rules that even now regulate eastern monasticism and inspired the development of this institution in the West. He was also a great politician and capable thinker. Gregory of Nyssa was the younger and less practical brother, but, on a more speculative level, much more original. Of the three, he was the one who passionately furthered the development of the Trinitarian argument. Gregory Nazianzus was a friend of Basil, a fellow student in Athens who stands out for the quality of his expression and the vigor of his argumentation. The theological depth in his writings is admirable for its clarity and effectiveness. He also facilitated the spread of orthodox thought through the composition of hymns and theological poetry.

The historical moment in which they found themselves enabled them to choose a point of entry into the Mystery of God that was complementary to that of Athanasius. The latter began his approach from the unity of the essence and moved toward the distinction of the three divine Persons. Instead, the Cappadocian Fathers started out from the three Persons and recognized their perfect unity of essence and nature through a deep study of what had been revealed. For this, it was essential to have recourse to a distinction between *ousia* and *hypostasis*—two terms which, as we have already seen, were still considered to be synonymous at Nicaea and in Athanasius. This can easily be seen in the fact that *hypostasis* is translated into Latin literally as *sub-stantia*—that is, with the same term that *ousia* takes in translation. This coincidence caused a peculiar difficulty when speaking of the three *hypostases* of the Father, Son and Holy Spirit, for that might have been understood in the sense of three different substances, and thus in the Arian sense of the term. The proposal to distinguish the terms *ousia* and *hypostasis* was advanced at the council of Alexandria in 362, where an attempt was made to attribute to the latter term a dimension that was strictly personal.

The Cappadocian Fathers developed this distinction and came to a description of the Trinity as a *single ousia and three hypostases*— a formula that has the merit of contrasting the terms *ousia* and *hypostasis* by way of different numeric combinations, thereby excluding the possibility that they be understood as synonymous. Hence, it becomes evident that *ousia* and *hypostasis* are answers to different questions: If one asks *what is* the Trinity, the answer is, one single *ousia,* the divine nature, the unique, eternal, and uncreated nature; but, if one asks instead *who* and not *what,* the answer is, the three *hypostases* of the Father, Son and Holy Spirit. In this way, the formula avoids an inappropriate reduction of the Trinity to unity, as in the case of Sabellius and the Modalists when they maintained the notion of a single *hypostasis* with three "masks". This formula also prohibits the breakdown of the substance of the Trinity as seen in the doctrine of Arius.

The apparently paradoxical combination of *one* and *three* opens up the possibility of considering a dimension of being that could never be known save through revelation. In fact, the unity of the three divine Persons cannot be understood as that of three representatives of a species that are distinguished among themselves only on the basis of accidental characteristics. The Father, Son and Holy Spirit not only *have* the same substance but they *are* the same substance, numerically identical. When we look at an individual human being, we do not see the entirety of human nature; by contrast, when we contemplate the Son we see the entirety of the divine substance in that each Person is *fully* God.

This means that the relation between the Father and the Son is a relation of total self-gift. The first Person does not give to the second a part of Himself, a portion of His being or His power; rather, He gives all of Himself, the whole of his divinity. Thus springs forth the Holy Spirit, who, precisely because of this, is the Spirit of the Father and the Spirit of the Son. In a beautiful expression found in Letter 38 among Basil's epistles, though probably written by Gregory of Nyssa, one reads, "In them there is an ineffable mystery of communion and distinction" (PG 32, 332).

Unity and trinity are found together, a unity that is no longer a oneness of isolation, like the ancient monolith that was considered sacred in the more primitive pagan religions. Nor is it the unity of an organism, where the various parts relate to one another in order to sustain an integral whole. Here, instead, each Person is not the part but the whole, and each one is Himself in relation to the other two—Being is communion.

In the thought of the Cappadocians, the ineffability of this mystery is extremely important. They had to confront Eunomius who developed and refined Arian doctrine. For Eunomius, every name corresponded to an essence, thereby rendering the Father and the Son ontologically different inasmuch as they had different names. If the Father was not generated (*agénnetos*) whereas the Son was generated, it meant they could not really be the same thing.

Two related problems converge in this claim: A) the lack of distinction between the two different meanings of "un-generated"; B) and a conception of "generation" that is only natural and material.

A) Regarding the term *un-generated*, it can be taken in the sense of the relation between God and the world, in a way equivalent to *not created*. However, it can also be understood with reference to God in His immanence, in his intimate and eternal dimension, where the term indicates *not being generated* by another divine Person. The Son is not created, and so, like the Father, is un-generated in the first sense, but the Son is *generated* in the Trinitarian immanence and so is not *un-generated* like the Father in the second sense of the term.

All of this was not abstract; rather, it was born out of the need to understand on an exegetical level the passages of the New Testament that referred to the humanity of Christ—Christ who was hungry, suffered, and even died. The Arians attributed these passages to the *Logos* as second Person of the Trinity—and not to the incarnate *Logos*, that is to the human nature He assumed—thus deducing his inferiority with respect to the Father because it could not be that God would die. They did not succeed in recognizing two natures in Jesus, who was capable of carrying out actions that only God could accomplish—such as pardoning sins and raising Lazarus from the dead—while at the same time being fully human.

B) This implied a lack of clarity in the distinction between the *inside* and the *outside* of the Trinity. Being and action were confused, projecting into the immanence of the Trinity terms whose understanding was drawn from the created world. There was a second problem. The expression *generated* was understood, as Arius had understood it, according to natural categories. When applied to God, it was not purified as it ought to have been, stripped of every limitation and ontological or chronological difference.

This is why the Cappadocian Fathers strongly insist on *apophaticism*, or the claim that substances cannot be expressed in words. The sphere of language is different from that of being—one can speak of God in his being, but only starting with His action. Man cannot know being in an immediate way, and his concepts do not contain being itself within themselves. However, one can gain an idea of being through action, just as the smell in a now empty jug leads one to think that prior to that moment it was filled with wine (Gregory of Nyssa, *Canticum,* GNO VI, 36.12–38.2). Gregory of Nyssa, for example, challenged Eunomius on this, writing to him that if one cannot even define the nature of an ant, how can one claim to understand God? (*Contra Eunomium* III, GNO II, 238.19–20). Apophaticism is not an attitude that debases or undermines language and the force of reason, but rather draws attention to the depth of being and God Himself. This depth implies that all true knowledge of God and of reality is attained only through wonder (*Contra Eunomium* III; GNO II, 187. 9–11).

Hence, reason alone cannot know the immanence and the Trinity of God, but only his existence and his unity in that the Persons always act together with respect to the world. Nevertheless, once they are encountered in divine revelation, they can be recognized through their personal characteristics which leave a distinctive mark on their common acting. In fact, each of these actions has its origin in the Father, is realized by the Son and is brought to perfect completion in the Holy Spirit. To take an extremely limited example, one might liken this to a child who receives a gift from one of his friends, something he really likes but that no one knew about but this friend, and also, at the same time, a gift that is extremely expensive so it is clear that the father of this friend was the one who bought it. Furthermore, this gift is so well wrapped and decorated that it cannot but be the work of the mother's hand. The gift is one, but, for a person who already knows the people who prepared it, it is possible to recognize their involvement. From the act, therefore, one can move to being, not in an immediate way but rather passing through the personal and relational dimension, that is, through revelation.

It is precisely this last aspect that is the most important contribution in the reflections of the Cappadocian Fathers. They find themselves confronted with the need to distinguish the three Persons in God, yet without having recourse to essence, which according to classical philosophy identified being. The Father, Son and Holy Spirit are the same thing. How, then, can they be three if they are equal in all things? The answer lies in relation. We are talking about passing on to a new ontological plane, one that Greek metaphysics never knew: Beyond essence, there is another ontological principle, which is itself also original, and that is relation. For Aristotle, relation was an accident. In Greek, it was indicated with *pros ti,* that is, being turned toward something, referring to something else. It was simply an arrow that connected the substance to some other being. Thus, it immediately speaks of multiplicity and cannot be predicated of the First Principle toward which all things are oriented but that in itself is not oriented toward anything because it has no need of anything. Here, one notes a philosophical concept of relation that necessarily opposes perfection and love, absolute power and self-gift.

The ontological conception that emerges from Trinitarian doctrine in the fourth century and later perfected by Augustine is very different. The Father is distinct from the Son precisely because his name and his Person belong to the realm of relation. Speaking of God, this cannot be understood in an accidental sense, but nor in a substantial sense, otherwise one would undermine the unity and end up in Arianism. The Father, indeed, speaks of relation—to the Son. The former cannot be Himself without the latter, and the latter cannot be Himself without the former; and this reciprocal relation is not determined by necessity but is marked by the purest freedom of love: The Father is Himself in the giving of himself to the Son; and the Son is the image of the Father, and so it is He Himself who gives Himself back to the Father. The obedience that was proof of inferiority for the Arians shows itself instead to be the key to understanding the Trinitarian mystery inasmuch as free obedience constitutes communion. As Cardinal Schönborn writes, "In truth, what the Son Himself has shown us is profoundly paradoxical, that is, the fact that he is at once obedient in all things to the Father and united in all things with Him. In God there is no domination of the superior over the inferior—obedience is identical to freedom, the total gift of self is identical with full possession of one's self" (Schönborn, *L'icôn du Christ,* Paris: Cerf, 1986, 53).

The three divine Persons are the singular divine nature precisely in their mutual being in relation, One for the Other and One through the Other. This is a summit in the formulation of the Trinitarian mystery, which will later receive the name *perichoresis* although it is already perfectly delineated in the realm of Cappadocian doctrine. One can see ever more clearly why God is one *because* he is triune: The infinitely perfect being of God is the eternal dynamic communion of the divine Persons who, as mutual relations, eternally give of Themselves, One to the Other.

The Holy Spirit and the First Council of Constantinople

In the last decades of the fourth century, the harvest of the fruits of labor from various figures regarding the development of the doctrine of the third Person. We are brought to a definitive formulation of the Trinitarian dogma in the First Council of Constantinople in 381 where the divinity of the Holy Spirit was defined.

The divinity of the Holy Spirit has always been accepted without question in the Church in that the third Person is the Spirit of the Father and the Spirit of the Son. In fact, in conformity with Christ's command, Christians have always been baptized in the name of the three divine Persons.

Around the year 360, however, when a resolution to the problem of the divinity of the Son began to take hold on the level of theology, a new difficulty reared its head—the question of the divinity of the Holy Spirit. Here, the point of contention was the connection between generation and identity of nature owing to the need to make a deeper study of the procession of the Spirit. The latter, in fact, was not generated and therefore seemed unfit to claim to possess the same nature as the Father. The heresies in this area have a three-fold origin:

1. *Arianism.* The denial of the Son's divinity also implies *a fortiori* a denial of that of the Spirit. As the Son was the first creation of the Father, the Spirit had to have been the first creation of the Son.

2. *Egyptian Tropici.* This heresy, mentioned by Athanasius, recognizes the divinity of the second Person but denies the divinity of the third on the basis of the following argument: if the Spirit is God, He is such by birth, but then He is the son of the Son and has the Father for a *grandfather*. They confuse the third Person with an angel, interpreting several texts of the

Old Testament in reference to him which clearly relate him to the natural wind, as indicated by the very term (*Amos* 4:13).

3. *The Eastern Pneumatomachians, or Macedonians.* These claimed that nowhere does the Bible state that the Spirit is Creator. Hence, the world would not have been created by Him or through Him but only *in* Him. The third Person is, in fact, the Sanctifier and not the Creator. In the same line as the Tropici they proved the alleged absurdity of the divinity of the Spirit affirming that it would lead to an absurd conclusion: Either the Father is grandfather of the Spirit, or that the Jesus is not the only-begotten as the third Person should be His brother.

Initially, Athanasius and Basil were distinguished in their defence of the divinity of the third Person. The former demonstrated to the Tropici that the Holy Spirit cannot be part of creation inasmuch as the actions that are attributed to Him in Scripture are proper to God. Hence, His nature must be the single, eternal nature that is identified with the three Persons. For his part, Basil defended the divinity of the third Person starting from the liturgy, maintaining that, in conformity with the baptismal formula, one needs to adore the Spirit along with the Father and the Son. In fact, the Macedonians rejected the formula of the *Gloria,* maintaining that one could not say "Glory be to the Father and to the Son and to the Holy Spirit." That is, one could not put all three Persons on the same level. Being the prudent bishop that he was, Basil never used the term *consubstantial* for the Holy Spirit, looking instead for equivalent expressions that would be accepted more easily. However, he appealed to the same soteriological argument that Athanasius had used for the Son: If the Spirit is the giver of life, and this life is not that of God, then we have not been truly saved.

Both Athanasius and Basil died before the Council of Constantinople, convened by the Emperor Theodosius in 381 as a council of the East and only recognized as ecumenical in 451 by the Council of Chalcedon. The most recent research attributes to Gregory of Nyssa and Gregory Nazianzus a preponderant role in the composition of the section in the Creed devoted to the third Person. They had the time to deepen the pneumatological reflection. Gregory Nazianzus succeeded in distinguishing the procession of the Spirit from the generation of the Son, even indicating it with the name *ekpóreusis,* a term coined *ex novo* from the Greek verb used in John 15:26. For his part, Gregory of Nyssa elaborated upon a response that was highly effective with the Macedonians: Given that they accepted the divinity of the Son, but denied that of the Spirit, Gregory showed how the Spirit is not simply to be thought of as the mediating figure between the second Person and the world, but rather between the Father and the Son. In fact, the Son is Son inasmuch as He is the perfect Image of the Father, and so He is King as the Father is King. However, to be King implies possession of the Kingdom, and the Father gives the Son, precisely, His eternal Kingdom, which in turn the Son offers back to the Father. According to Gregory, this Kingdom is the Holy Spirit (*Adversos Macedonianos,* GNO III/1.102.26–28). In the same way, he claims that the Spirit is the Glory that the first two Persons eternally exchange between themselves. He is, then, their bond of union: The Father is Himself in giving glory to the Son, and the Son is Himself in rendering the glory back to the Father, yet, parallel to the Kingdom, this glory is identified with the third Person (*Canticum,* GNO VI, 467.2–17). The Spirit Himself is interpreted as Person-relation who is the basis of the intra-Trinitarian communion and projects it outward so that everything might be one just like the Father and the Son (*Jn* 17:21). This solution is extremely important because it shows how the two processions are interconnected—the Son is generated by the Father and gives Himself back to the Father precisely in the Holy Spirit, whose procession consists of being what is eternally exchanged between the first two Persons.

This theological advancement allowed for an extremely rich and effective expression of the divinity of the third Person at Constantinople. The primary addition made to the Nicaean Creed was in the article devoted to the Holy Spirit, who is now called "Lord". Even though, like the Scriptures, the text does not literally refer to him as God, the term Lord is very clear, for it is the translation of *Yahweh* in the Greek version of the Old Testament. Furthermore, it is said that He is "giver of life" with reference to His role as creator and re-creator. The life communicated by Him comes from the Father from whom *He proceeds,* something that is said explicitly. Therefore, the third Person is not un-generated like the Father, nor is He generated like the Son, but is still God in that He proceeds from the Father in eternity and is not created in time like all other beings. This is precisely why, taking up Basil's argument, the Spirit "is worshipped and glorified" with the Father and with the Son. This claim is reinforced through the careful repetition of the Greek prefix that serves as the English equivalent of the word "with". At Nicaea, a single term was not enough to assure the acknowledgment of the divinity of the Son. Thus, at Constantinople, it was decided to have recourse to a series of converging arguments that would not allow for any misinterpretation.

It is noticeable that the claim of the full divinity of the Spirit, and therefore also of his being Creator, has immediate consequences on any conception of the world. Given that the third Person pours forth His holiness, His role in the visible creation means that the world, even in its material nature, can be considered a place of encounter with God. It is profaned by sin, but is not profane in and of itself—there is always something holy to be found. This is the wonderful foundation of the universal call to holiness and the possibility of sanctifying daily realities and one's own work. From this perspective, it is significant that it was precisely at Constantinople that Mary was inserted into the Profession of Faith of the whole Church in a definitive way.

4. The Development of Thought: Theology

Theological Elaboration

Trinitarian dogma reached its full formulation in the fourth century. The Church solemnly proclaimed the divinity of the Son and the Spirit and, from then on, any future development of theological understanding had to move along the basis of these truths. However, the Mystery itself, in its full depth, remains inexhaustible. Hence subsequent centuries continued to offer a magnificent series of contributions that lead us to continue to marvel all the more at the one and triune God. It may be helpful to consider an analogy to better understand this phenomenon. If we think of dogma as though it were a sacred icon, then the theological contribution of the fourth century might be likened to the time when the canons regarding iconography were being established for any representation of the Trinity. Technique and artistic elaboration can only contribute, greatly increasing the beauty of icons. This is precisely the task of theology.

Augustine

One of the greatest theological contributions comes to us from Augustine, the greatest of the Fathers of the Latin Church. His work can be considered one of the pillars of the whole of Western thought. He was born in Thagaste, Africa, in 354. After having subscribed to various philosophical doctrines like Manichaeism and scepticism, he converted to Christianity in 386, in Milan, while listening to the sermons of Ambrose. Returning to Africa, he was ordained a priest in the year 391 in Hippo and was subsequently elected bishop of that city where he died in 430 during the siege of the Vandals. He wrote the majority of his works during the last thirty years of his life.

Augustine's theological study has its basis in what can be called interiority. When he searched for God through the external world, nothing satisfied his question; rather, all of his experience led him to search within himself (*Confessions* 10, 6, 9). In the end, we see him seeking the path to God in the very depths of his own soul.

This move is quite unsettling if we compare it with the background of ancient culture and literature where personal feelings were always concealed behind form and ideas. One thinks of the lack of fear that both Socrates and Antigone displayed at the prospect of death. The Gospel stands in stark contrast to them with the anguish of Christ and the inner turmoil of Mary. The Psalms are a unique example in literary history for they present an innocent victim, unjustly persecuted, crying out to God from his innermost self. This scriptural heritage gave Augustine the tools to develop his thought with regard to the interiority of the human person in a way that had never been seen before and allowed him to base the entirety of his theology precisely on this.

When man turns inward, addressing his interiority, he discovers within himself the ideas of knowledge, justice, truth, etc., which refer back to God as their origin and source. These eternal truths that are present in us, within our thoughts and wills, allow us to brush against perfection within ourselves even though we ourselves are imperfect. In the depths of himself, man finds a way to Him who is the source of every good, true and beautiful reality. Here, we are not talking about escaping what is limited, but rather of going into the depths, for God is so great as to let Himself be found even there.

At the root of Augustine's approach, there is a theory of knowledge that follows the Platonic tradition, re-examined from a Christian perspective. The light by which man knows anything is divine light because the eternal truths that are infused in his soul through illumination originate in God whose essence is identified with Beauty, Goodness and Truth. Therefore, the human soul is also a way of accessing the Trinity inasmuch as it bears the image of the Trinity. In fact, man possesses a mind (*mens*) from which springs knowledge (*notitia*), and this knowledge moves him to love (*amor*). This is a development of the theology of the *Logos,* which is now complete with the reference to the will. Hence, the thinking and willing of humans are now interpreted as essential elements of the 'image' of the Trinity and can become a way of accessing it.

This doctrine is known as *psychological analogy* because it recognizes the image of the Trinity in man at the level of the relations among his spiritual faculties. The capacity to think and to love stems directly from the fundamental relationship between man and God and points directly toward the immanence of the Trinity.

With this analogy, Augustine is able to give an account of both the unity and trinity of God. Just as the soul of man is one yet with three distinct realities—the mind, intellect and will—so it is with God. Here, Augustine is not superimposing lower concepts on to a higher reality, attributing the composition of human beings to the Trinity, but mounting a useful argument to show how, on the basis of what man can know of himself, being both one and triune is not actually so absurd. The foundation for this is biblical. Augustine simply refers to the creation of man as God's image and likeness in Genesis 1:26.

Elaborating on the matter from this perspective, Augustine is able to distinguish the two processions of the Son and the Spirit, connecting the first with how knowledge proceeds from the mind and the second with how the will is moved toward the thing that is known. These processions do not multiply God's essence in that they are immanent, that is, they do not go out of God but remain *in* Him. The Spirit is thus presented as the bond that unites the Father and the Son, and is explicitly identified with the Love that they eternally exchange. He is the communion of the Father and the Son, Their Relation, which is not merely an accident in the philosophical sense of the term but is here identified with the third divine Person. On this issue, Eastern theology was of a more sober perspective. It refrained from using similar existential and anthropological language largely on account of the polemical context in which it was developed. With his conception of interiority, however, Augustine succeeded in coming much closer to the mystery of the human being by having recourse to those dimensions, such as that of the will, whose value was acknowledged precisely on account of revelation.

In the context of the psychological analogy, the procession of the Holy Spirit comes from both the Father and the Son because the will always comes after an act of the intellect: One cannot truly love what one does not know. Then, the identification of the third Person as the bond between the first two presses us toward this conclusion. This is the issue of the *Filioque*, which characterized Western theology from the beginning. The term means *and from the Son*, to indicate that the Spirit does not proceed from the Father alone, but *also* from the second Person. As we shall see later on, this will become a cause of the division between East and West.

It must be said that, in Augustine's time, Greek and Latin theologians knew each other, and the differences in terminology and approach were accepted and understood. The Bishop of Hippo specified that the Holy Spirit proceeds from the Father alone if one understands the procession from the point of view of its *ultimate principle*, indicating this with the adverb "principally" (*principaliter*), whereas one can also say that the third Person proceeds from the Father and the Son in the sense of their communion (*communiter*), that is, their bond of love (*De Trinitate*, 15, 17, 29). We could use as an example the construction of the transcontinental railroad in the United States. Before 1860 the only ways to cross from the East to the West Coast were either by sea through the Cape Horn route or by train to St. Louis, Missouri, and by wagon after that point. Both solutions took at least a few months. When the railroad was completed, it became possible to start the journey in New York and go all the way to Sacramento, California, via St. Louis. Augustine's *principaliter* expresses the starting point, i.e. the ultimate origin of the procession of the Holy Spirit, while his *communiter* asserts that the third Person is also from the Son, just as a train from New York arrived in Sacramento *via* St. Louis.

An essential element to understanding Augustine's perspective is his metaphysical analysis of the category of relation. In God, this category is not substance, yet nor is it accident inasmuch as everything in God is eternal. Creatures *have* relation, but they can also *not* have it, and the relations themselves can mutate and change. The Trinity, however, *is* three eternal relations because the Father is relation to the Son, the Son is relation to the Father, and the Spirit is relation to both. Thus Augustine concludes that "these appellations do not belong to the order of substance but to relation; and relation that is not an accident because it does not change" (*De Trinitate*, 5, 5, 6). Thus, the discovery of the non-accidental relation is formalized, and it is a distinct characteristic of an ontology that has been renewed by the Trinitarian revelation. Christian thought increasingly assumes a definite identity that refers to relation, the person and the communion of love.

The Spirit of the Middle Ages

The power of Augustinian thought was to be the drive behind the whole of Latin reflection, and in some way it foreshadowed the Middle Ages with its tendency to provide synthesis and a vision of the whole, accompanied by the attention given to man and his spirit.

With the increasing comprehension of the revealed Truth combined with theological development, a gradual demand arose not only to operate in a Christian culture like that of the Fathers, but to do so in such a way that civilization itself became its reflection. This meant that every aspect of human life and society was to be placed in a definite position of relation to God, the center around which all reality revolved. The medieval city is a visible example of this spirit, with its cathedral in the center and the seat of civil power next to it, and all the various quarters moving outward from these, often segregated according to the various crafts and trades. Everything had its proper place. In all its completeness, the medieval *Summa* is the result of this way of thinking.

The risk of this approach, however, was that of forcing this interpretation to find the appropriate position for every reality. This drove forward an extension of the use of the metaphor as attempts were made to give a complete picture. But this implied the danger of forgetting the moment in which the purely analogical dimension is to be abandoned. It is the difference between saying *the bread is good*, where goodness is really experienced and comes from God who is Goodness itself, and saying that a man is *as good as bread*, where the parallel has a basis in reality but might also be expressed in another way.[9] For example, in a part of the world where there is no grain, this phrase would be incomprehensible. In fact, one has moved from the level of *being* to that of *interpretation*. And this is not always explicit, as when we say, "You're a sweetheart" to communicate a kind of goodness about someone. It is obvious that we do not actually mean that his physical heart is sweet. What is in-

9 Translator's Note: The Italian idiom used here, "to be good like bread", is equivalent to the English expression "to be as good as gold".

tended is only an implied comparison. The Church Fathers were theologically apophatic precisely in order to protect the analogical dimension of theology by making quite clear the meaning and limits of metaphors, which are evidently very useful when speaking of God.

All these contributing elements must be kept in mind when approaching the doctrine of Anselm of Canterbury (†1109), and in particular his ontological argument. He intended his theological work as a contemplation and praise of God, accomplished by way of rational research. He perceived theology as faith seeking understanding (*fides quaerens intellectum*). It was within this context that his attempt to prove the existence of God, the so-called ontological argument, was born. In a nutshell, it starts from the premise that every man possesses the concept of God as the most perfect being that can be imagined, but, as existence is itself a perfection, so it cannot be that the One who is the sum of all perfections does not exist. Therefore, God must exist (*Proslogion* 2–3).

The difficulty in accepting this 'proof' lies in the movement from the order of logic to the order of what is real. This is why Thomas Aquinas rejects it. In order to evaluate Anselm's thought, one should consider the fact that he worked within the Augustinian tradition, and stated explicitly that this argument applies only to the concept of God.

If one keeps in mind what has been said about the medieval spirit of seeking the vision of the whole, one can see the limits of this kind of proof. In fact, today, this proof would have little to contribute in moving human beings closer to God. Anselm operates in a context in which the experience and knowledge of God are so greatly shared by all that the premises which serve as a point of departure for his ontological argument are attributed such strength as to lead necessarily to the conclusion of the existence of God. In itself, this indicates a very positive climate for the faith. At the same time, however, the situation ran the risk of blurring the boundaries between the natural and the supernatural. One might forget the area where reason is admitted only as a result of revelation, that is, only on the merit of the divine gift, because the civilization in which one lives is saturated with this gift.

Something similar happens with the claim that everything is identical within the Trinity, with no allowance for relative opposition (*omnia sunt idem ubi non obviat relationis oppositio*). The Father is identical with the essence, just as the Son is, but the Father is not the Son. The fact of their relation excludes it. The two terms of a real relation cannot coincide—that is, one cannot be the father of himself. This particular formula was to be adopted by the Magisterium at the Council of Florence (1431–1445). At the same time, however, Anselm considers it to be a true axiom of reality, and thus runs the risk of forgetting that it is derived from revelation and an understanding of salvation history, without which it would have been impossible to arrive at the Trinity.

Richard of Saint Victor (†c. 1173) found himself in a similar situation. He belonged to the school of Saint Victor, founded at the beginning of the twelfth century by William of Champeaux in an old abbey near Paris where there was a search for a synthesis between science and mysticism. He wrote an important treatise, *De Trinitate*, in which the influence of both Augustine and Anselm is clear. His doctrine on the Trinity is constructed in a unique way according to the Augustinian intuition that love demands otherness as a result of which the Trinity is represented as Lover, Beloved and Love.

The *De Trinitate* can be outlined in the following manner: It begins at the observational level of created beings and, according to classical philosophical proofs of order and beauty, deduces the existence of the divine essence, uncreated substance without accidents (chapter one). However, this substance is Love, and Love requires the presence of someone else, so the divine Persons must number at least two. Moreover, these Persons must possess equal dignity, for one truly loves only that which is worthy of being loved (chapter two). Additionally, perfect love is reciprocal love. However, the happiness that comes from this love has an intrinsic desire to be communicated, so that They who love both desire to have Someone to whom to communicate this love, and the desire must be likewise shared. Hence, there must be a beloved in common (*Condilectus*), and the Persons must be three so that the love be perfect (chapter three). From here, Richard advances a very original definition of the person having recourse to the concept of existence (chapter four), and concludes by identifying the three Persons as the Father, the Son and the Holy Spirit (chapter six).

He guides the reader along this beautiful path to the Trinity, one argument at a time, beginning by showing how *being* is understood as Love. His vigorous and synthetic thought is an attempt to deduce the Trinity from the infinite perfection of God. Unfortunately, Richard too runs the risk of downplaying the role of faith. He unintentionally introduces necessary reasons for divine love and constructs a system in which Fatherhood and Sonship do not appear to be more than the culmination of a logical argument. Richard deemed his arguments irresistible but, subsequently, along with Anselm, they drew the criticism of Thomas Aquinas. This does not, however, diminish the great mystical value of his thought, which clearly represents an essential moment in the development of Trinitarian theology.

The Synthesis of Thomas Aquinas

Thomas Aquinas was born in Roccasecca, Italy, in the year 1224. After his studies in Naples, he entered the Dominican order and studied at Cologne with Albert the Great. During the course of his life he taught in Cologne, Paris and Naples. On December 6, 1273, he suddenly stopped writing after a mystical experience, and, on March 7 of the following year, he died while traveling to the Council of Lyons.

His work is like a magnificent cathedral that is simultaneously a place for adoration and a display of the inexhaustible riches of the mystery. The heart of his theology is mystical, but this interiority opens itself up to the entirety of creation and to all people in order to draw all to Christ. His attitude is deeply catholic—in the etymological sense of the term—and this is reflected in his methodology. At times, his writings can be exhausting to the modern reader who is more accustomed to reaching practical conclusions immediately. But this is because Aquinas always analyzes the arguments of his predecessors. He embodies what G.K. Chesterton called the *democracy of the dead*: He does not act like a genius who censures his predecessors or strikes up a dialectical relationship with them. Instead, he considers every school of reasoning and takes account of every difference. His method appears to be profoundly relational. In this way, his theology is rendered timeless despite the need to incorporate or accommodate data acquired through reflection in subsequent historical periods. His conclusions can be extended because he left tracks that one can follow like a kind of narrative on the path he himself once trod. That is why the Church labels his theology as a fundamental reference.

His doctrine of the Trinity reached its most complete formulation in the *Summa Theologiae*. The first twenty-six questions are dedicated to the unity of God and, therefore, to what one can know about God through reason alone. The part that explicitly engages the concept of the Trinity is laid out in the subsequent seventeen questions (*ST* I, 27–43). This distinction is extremely important in that it marks the area of thought that is accessible through revelation alone. The medieval tendency toward synthesis is, then, counterbalanced by the attention given to the inexhaustible depth of the mystery. The distinction between the section on God as one and that on God as triune has the function of protecting the divine Gift, avoiding the error of thinking that what only a personal relationship can give might instead be the fruit of necessary reasoning. This is why Aquinas emphasizes the negative (apophatic) dimension of theology, stating that we cannot speak of what God *is*, but only of what God *is not* (*ST* I, 3). Thomas, therefore, reiterates that the rational arguments proposed by Anselm and Richard do not have probative force, but are only mere congruencies which can be identified *a posteriori*. The Trinity cannot be demonstrated (*ST* I, 32, ad 1, ad 2; also *In Boetium*, 1, ad 4). In fact, *creatures lead us to the knowledge of God, as an effect points to its cause* (*ST* I, 32, ad 1), and everything the Trinity accomplishes through creation is common to all three Persons and cannot be used to distinguish Them without revelation. If this point is clear, one can proceed to the use of analogy, and read in the different degrees of reality how the actions of God have touched all things.

For Thomas, understanding a theological truth does not mean demonstrating it rationally, something impossible *per se*, but with simultaneous recourse to faith and reason recognizing how, through participation, that truth leaves its mark on the different levels of reality, according to analogy. Faithful to the patristic legacy, Aquinas aims toward the contemplation of the Trinity itself, the final end of man. Hence, the key to understanding the whole of the treatise on the Trinity is the awareness that it ends with the treatment of the indwelling of the Trinity in the human soul. Through the theology of the missions, everything converges in the presentation of the Christian faith as a message of salvation for all human beings.

In constructing his treatise, Thomas chooses to start from the processions (question 27), and moves on to analyze relations (question 28), ending with a structured study of the Persons. It culminates in the identification of the Persons themselves with the three eternal relations of Fatherhood, Sonship and Spiration. To explain this, one must begin with the fact that the names revealing the Trinity in the Gospels imply two processions: In order for there to be the Son, it is necessary that He proceeds through the generation by the Father, that is, that he has his origin from Him. The same goes for the Spirit of whom it is said explicitly that he proceeds from the Father (*Jn* 15:26).

Therefore, procession indicates the origin that one being has through another. We can distinguish two types of procession: movement out from the subject—called transient—and movement remaining interior to the subject—called immanent. For example, an image that I conceive of in my mind is distinct from me and proceeds from me, and yet it remains in me if I do not express it. In this case, it is immanent. However, if I decide to draw that image, then it proceeds outside of me, and the drawing is thereby the product of a transient procession.

If we consider these categories when approaching Scripture, we realize that we must speak of both types of processions when we speak of God. The event of creation is clearly a transient procession whereas the generation of the Son and the procession of the Holy Spirit are immanent processions. Naturally, in this case, we must purge any element of movement from potency to act from the concept of procession, as well as any reference to time or motion, and leave only the pure relationship of origin.

The concept of immanent procession is key because it allows for an expression of the being of God as one and triune without multiplying His essence. In fact, procession implies distinction because what proceeds must be different than that from which it proceeds, just as the image I have in my mind is truly distinct from me as I think of it. Yet at the same time, immanence implies unity, for the end of the procession does not leave the essence alone by itself. Arius did not accept the unity of substance of the Father and the Son in his theology, inasmuch as he regarded the eternal generation as a transient procession.

Taking Scripture as his point of departure, Thomas developed the conceptual instrument of the immanent procession in order to make a faithful formulation of the mystery of the one and triune God. From here, he moves to the actions that bring about the two processions of the Son and the Spirit—to the two immanent processions there must correspond two immanent operations, which are purely spiritual and eternal, void of the faintest hint of movement or imperfection. Here, he makes use of the legacy of Augustine, which leads him to identify these two operations as knowing and loving, in accordance with what likewise happens in the human spirit. This allows one to distinguish the individual processions of the Son and the Spirit. The former proceeds in an analogical way with how thought proceeds from the mind, in conformity with the name *Logos* used in the Gospel. The third Person, instead, originates in an analogical way with the procession of love.

The perfection of the processions requires that the Person who is proceeding be identified with the very substance in which the process is immanent, just as the more perfectly a thing is understood the more it is one thing with the individual who understands (*ST* I, 27, ad 1, ad 2). The Son and the Spirit are one with the Father; they are the one and only divine substance.

The transition from the two processions to the affirmation of the unity and trinity of God is achieved through a conceptual instrument that is especially powerful in Thomas: relation. In fact, each of the two immanent processions constitutes a pair of opposite relations, making a total of four relations in God. Generation establishes paternity and sonship, for He who generates is identified with the first, and He who is generated with the second. Two opposite relations exist in the procession of the spiration of the Holy Spirit to which no corresponding equivalent name exists at the level of creation, unlike the procession of the Son. These two processions are called *active spiration* and *passive spiration*. Here, the adjective "passive" is used only to indicate the relation of origin because in itself nothing is passive in God. Even when saying that the Son is generated by the Father, one does not mean that the second Person submits, rather that both the Father and the Son are active.

Of these four relations, however, only three are real and distinct, interacting with each other and constituting the divine Persons—Fatherhood, Sonship and passive Spiration. It is impossible to be both father and son to oneself, just as it is impossible to be simultaneously spirated and spirate. Yet it is indeed possible to be Father and spirate, and to be Son and spirate in that the relations are interrelated and not in opposition to one another. This is how one acknowledges that in God there exist three eternal relations––and not four––all truly distinct from each other, inasmuch as active spiration is not distinguishable from Fatherhood and Sonship. In God, these relations are not accidental. They are God himself, they *are* the divine substance.

In Thomistic theology, it is precisely these relations that are critical to any demonstration of the fact that what we believe is a mystery, and that we are not affirming an absurdity. These relations show that God is one *because* He is triune, not *in-spite-of-being* triune. Whereas in nature man knows relations only as accidents— that is, as a reality that cannot exist without a substance to inhere in or attach to—in the Trinity, the relations exist in themselves, for they are identified with the fullness of the purely substantial being of God. In technical terms, we say that the divine Persons are three *subsisting* relations. Hence the Father is pure fatherhood, the Son is pure sonship, and the Holy Spirit is pure spiration, that is, relation to the first two divine Persons from whom He proceeds.

In this way, the relations in God are truly distinct from each other which is why the three Persons of the Trinity exist. Yet, at the same time, each of them—inasmuch as they are subsisting— is identified with the eternal, simple and infinite substance of God. Thus, the distinction between substance and relations in God is only one of human reasoning in the sense that we are talking about a single reality in which distinction is perceptible only on the level of our own thought. To elucidate further using another analogy, a priest who is also a professor of theology is only identified separately as being a priest or being a professor in our minds.

Thus, the Thomas Aquinas' Trinitarian doctrine leads to the acknowledgement that, in *one* God, the claim that He is *triune* is due only to the relations and their reciprocal interaction. In this way, one avoids the risk of understanding essence as the subject of generation, an assertion made by Joachim of Fiore who was condemned in the Fourth Lateran Council (1215). There is no priority of essence over Personhood in the Trinity, rather the entirety of the divine Being is perfectly identified with the three eternal Relations constituted by the operations of Love and Knowledge.

The weight of this theological thought, firmly rooted in the work of the Church Fathers, makes Aquinas' contribution an essential point of reference for all subsequent theological development. As is true of any great teacher, the fruitfulness of his thought was to be reflected in the multitude of interpretations. Yet these would not always successfully preserve his original balance.

Subsequent Theology

Subsequent theological development was tied to what has been said of the spirit of the Medieval Period and the search for a rational development that might achieve a unified and comprehensive framework. This effort is especially evident in the work of John Duns Scotus (†1308). His primary interest shifts toward the concept of infinity, which assumes the place of Aquinas's subsisting Being. He identifies the nucleus of the divine Persons with incommunicability rather than with subsisting relation. He increases the number of distinctions to give new expression to all the most difficult questions in a philosophical and properly Christian language. Together with the subsequent loss of the apophatic dimension, this shift facilitated the rise of nominalism. This approach claims that the relationship between the names of things and their actual being is not governed by analogy. One can only say that something is good *like* bread, but one cannot say that bread *is* good in the sense that it participates in the Good.

With William of Ockham (†1349), the balance between reason and faith, thought and the will, is shattered in favour of the latter. Whereas relation and analogy had once facilitated comprehension of the harmonious relationship between faith and reason, with Ockham, a dialectical component inserts itself between them. With the genuine intention of demonstrating the greatness of God, he argues that things are good and moral only because God commands it to be so. God might say, then, that evil is good and good is evil. This is a clear departure from the Church Fathers, especially Origen, who, as previously seen, made it clear that God cannot deny his Being by doing evil. Nominalism, then, places more emphasis on authority than on authoritativeness.

This change shifted attention to the subject and the ego. The Augustinian legacy continued to mark the direction of Western thought, even though the late-medieval framework had deprived it of the attention given to mystery and being that characterized Augustine's brilliant synthesis. This was to have an enormous influence, and one important example of this is the Protestant Reformation.

Luther was, in fact, an Augustinian friar (†1546). He reacted against some of the excesses he saw in the ecclesiastical life and theology of his day, claiming that the God who saves ought to be central, as opposed to all the attention given to God in His Being. This led him to underscore once again the soteriological element that had characterized the living and existential thought of the Church Fathers. Yet, the *distinction* between the action of God and His being—which was essential to the formulation of Christian doctrine—was here replaced by a *separation* that was due to the influence of nominalism. Denial of metaphysical inquiry leads to the rejection of some of the most important dogmatic concepts and to a breach with ecclesial tradition. More specifically, Luther's claims that faith alone saves—independent of works (*sola fide*)—and that everyone must interpret Scripture for himself without the need of priestly mediation (*sola Scriptura*)—undermine the central role of *relation* in theological thought. And this is paradoxical because Luther himself was reacting against the lack of relational dimension that characterized classical metaphysics. In this new intellectual climate, philosophical development was to lead to both idealism and rationalism. Once faith and reason are divorced, the reasoning of the individual comes to assume center stage.

In this intellectual environment, on the theological front, Francisco Suarez (†1617) separated the treatise of God as one from the treatise of God as triune, although with the good intention of facilitating the discussion of philosophical questions concerning God. The aim was to encourage apologetics, that is, the defence of the faith through philosophical dialogue. The epistemological questions took precedence and those questions that were properly Trinitarian increasingly gave way to the problem of the knowledge of God. The Magisterium was compelled to address the situation. For example, *Dei Filius* (April 24, 1870) of the Vatican Council I is a response to fideism and rationalism.

This weakening of the distinction between the philosophical and the properly theological sphere led to a phenomenon typical of the modern era, and quite positive. Numerous philosophers showed an interest in the Trinity. In his *Essays on Theodicy*, for example Leibniz (†1716) attempts to demonstrate that no contradiction exists in the possibility of there being three Persons in the one God. In like manner, Fichte (†1814), Schelling (†1854) and, most importantly, Hegel (†1831) devoted attention to reflections on the Trinity.

Hegel's work is noteworthy in that he affirms the diffusion of the absolute spirit in history according to the threefold sequence of thesis, antithesis and synthesis. In this way, the dialectic achieves the height of its expression in his system. Using this key, he subjects Trinitarian theology to his imposing speculative reflection and analysis. Yet he falls short in his attempt to grasp the value of relation as it emerges from the history of dogma. In fact, according to Hegel, the synthesis needs to overcome both the thesis and the antithesis and simply replace them. Relation, on the contrary, unites its terms without eliminating them. In the dialectical approach, therefore, the concrete must yield before the advance of the absolute spirit—an idea that materialised as a tragic reality for the countless victims of totalitarian regimes in the twentieth century. By contrast, thought concerning relation holds the unique advantage of capturing the value of both the absolute as well as that of the individual and the person.

During the last century, in part as a reaction to the horrors that followed these developments, there was a strong aversion against idealism and rationalism with the affirmation of the primacy of the individual over everything that is universal and determined. This movement took the name of existentialism and had a powerful influence on theology, often assuming anti-metaphysical tones.

This was to be challenged in the twentieth century by the rediscovery of relation and communion as fundamental pillars of doctrine that relies on Revelation. There has been a great resurgence of Trinitarian studies, bound up also with four theological movements that redirected thought back to drink from the freshness of the sources of faith. The first movement is *biblical*, one that advocates the rediscovery of Sacred Scripture as the soul of theology. Linked with this is the parallel *liturgical* movement. Both have multiple points of contact with the *patristic* movement that seeks inspiration from the Church Fathers for the restoration of the vitality of theology that is derived from constant contact with the

Bible and the liturgy. Finally, the development of *ecumenism* presses in the same direction, leading to a deeper appreciation of the sources in order to rediscover the common roots of the various Christian confessions.

As examples, one might cite authors like Yves Congar (1904–1995), Hans Urs von Balthasar (1905–1988), Jean Daniélou (1905–1974), Louis Bouyer (1913–2004) and Henri de Lubac (1896–1991). Lubac, in his wonderful book *Catholicism: Christ and the Common Destiny of Man*—the first edition of which dates back to 1938—proposes a rereading of the entirety of Catholic dogma from the beginning, starting from the concept of communion, in order to show how it is characterized by an intrinsic social—and therefore relational—dimension. Joseph Ratzinger, too, can be linked to these movements through his theological treatment of the liturgy and his constant reference to Augustine.

In more strictly Trinitarian terms, the work of Michael Schmaus (1897–1993) is important with its immense wealth of Patristic sources. His manual brings together again the treatise on God as one with the treatise on God as triune, giving back primacy to a properly theological reading of the material. Karl Rahner (1904–1984) offers another remarkable contribution. He asks, provocatively, whether or not the ordinary Christian would be aware of any change if, *per absurdum*, the Trinity were to be removed from the Catechism. This is his reason for emphasizing the role of the individual divine Persons in the action of the Trinity. He maintains one fundamental principle (*Grundaxiom*)—namely, the Trinity in its saving action throughout history is the same Trinity of divine immanence, *and vice versa*. Here, Rahner means to emphasize how we enter into true relation with the three divine Persons, and how They truly enter into relation with us. The first part of the axiom is valid, yet it becomes problematic when it asserts that it also applies in the opposite direction—namely, that the Trinity's immanence is fully revealed in history. This actually endangers the dimension of mystery and, as in some developments of Augustinianism, blurs the boundaries between the natural and the supernatural dimensions. At present, most theologians reject the second part of Rahner's fundamental principle.

The Vatican Council II (1962–1965) brought together many of these historical movements. Strictly speaking, it was not a dogmatic council like Nicaea or Constantinople inasmuch as it did not add any dogmas to Trinitarian doctrine. It was primarily pastoral. The concern of bringing the Church into active dialogue with the world is manifested in its focus on showing that the life and work of the Church are rooted precisely in the Trinity, and therefore in the communal and personal dimension.

In view of all these developments, contemporary Trinitarian theology continues to grow in its interest in Trinitarian and relational ontology, for example as seen in the work of Piero Coda and John Milbank. In seeking to develop philosophical thought, their research confirms that the metaphysical newness constituted by the discovery that God, the subsisting Being, is simultaneously substance *and* relations. The personal communion of the Father, Son and Holy Spirit is the ontological foundation of all that exists.

5. The Trinitarian Conception of Man and the World

The Trinity and the World

Thus far, we have seen how the revelation of the Trinity has challenged man's thought, which through faith has been opened up toward a unity that is not solitude, but communion—a unity that is a trinity, not in a paradoxical sense, but as the foundation and source of all other unity. Classical philosophy could not comprehend it and therefore assumed a model of unity taken empirically from nature. Christian doctrine had to replace this model with that of the unity of the Father, of the Son and of the Holy Spirit.

In the question of the one and the triune, the relationship between God and the world is at stake. Theology has had to learn how not to reduce the Trinity to the categories of thought derived from natural observation, and instead to modify its own conceptual instruments so as to take account of the unimaginable Truth encountered in Christ. When this was accomplished, it became possible to go back and reread the world, beginning with its constitutive relationship with the Trinity itself.

To do this, however, it is necessary to think about being in an analogical sense because the world is not the Trinity. What is true for God does not necessarily apply to man. That is why, as has been seen repeatedly, to speak about the Triune God we must eliminate any linguistic references to movement, time or ontological difference. In fact, the heresies indicate critical moments of this process, moments that served as stimuli for further investigation and favored a purification of theological thought.

Pseudo-Dionysius, the Areopagite, a mysterious author of the fifth or sixth century, described the process of this development as three-fold. The first phase is constituted by the *affirmation* of some perfection of God or by the application to Him of a certain concept like procession or generation. This phase must be followed immediately by a second phase, which is a *negation* insofar as that reality is not present in God with the limits found in nature. This culminates in a final phase that acknowledges the *eminence* of God, in which He is recognized as the source of all partial realizations of that reality, though it is perfectly possessed by God and lies beyond any human conception. For example, if we affirm that God is great, we must simultaneously deny that He is 'great' in the material sense of the word, so as to then conclude that He is great inasmuch as He is the eternal source of every greatness. So, in a seemingly paradoxical way, we can also say that God is small because *being small* can be understood as perfection—here we might think of the possibility of nearness or being inside, something that smallness implies even at the material level. God is the source of *every perfection* so that one can purify smallness in such a way as to recognize God as its origin. That is why the divine attributes coincide with one another just as the rays of the sun converge and are unified in their source. God is, then, both small and great, and yet remains without contradiction.

The task of theology, therefore, consists in the development of thought that does not explain or reduce the Mystery but causes it to emerge in a formulation that is increasingly less *inadequate*. This happens when one is able to show a certain aspect of God as the source of perfections found in nature, and of those perfections recognized by philosophy and the other human sciences. That is why the essence of theology demands harmony with the other disciplines.

The work of the theologian must simultaneously maintain the presence of two extremes: a) The being of God belongs to a different ontological sphere from that of the world, a sphere that we can know only in part through what God has willed to reveal about Himself, but which we do not possess and experience directly; b) Creation reflects the perfections of its Creator, and man reflects this perfection to the utmost because he is created in the image and likeness of the Trinity itself.

Therefore, we must be very cautious when we attribute to God realities that have a specific realization on the natural level. For example, if being a father at the created level is impossible without the presence of a wife and mother, this does not mean that in God there must be a bride. At the same time, we must also bear in mind that the transition from God to the world cannot be equivocal, for what we have come to know in God through revelation is inevitably reflected as perfection in creation. A further example may clarify this: it is said that God does not *have* relations, rather *is* three eternal relations. We humans, on the other hand, have relations but we do not identify ourselves with our relations. Yet, for a human person, perfection should be found in his or her relations precisely because God is the source of every perfection. Hence, the father of a family will become himself much more fully by giving himself completely to his children, and therefore growing in his identification with his relation of fatherhood rather than through the achievement of extraordinary professional success if this distances him from his relations. Work is good when it serves fundamental relations but is negative when it distances one from them, regardless of any economic prosperity.

Persons and Relation

This vision is linked to the personal dimension which is the key to the formulation of the unity and trinity of God. One of the peaks of Trinitarian reflection has been the work done to achieve an adequate definition of the word "person" that can be applied analogically to both man and God.

We can see how in antiquity this concept was linked to multiplicity and imperfection, and so could not be applied to God. The early Fathers, such as Justin, were still affected by this difficulty when they stated that the Son is a person because He manifests Himself and enters into relation with man and creation whereas the Father cannot be a person.

Boethius (†525) offers the initial definition: *Individual substance of a rational nature* (*De duabus naturis*, 3). The fundamental element of his definition of person is substance which takes account of individuality. Here, he reflects the original identification of *ousia* and *hypostasis*, with an apparent equivalence of the latter to *substance*. Later, theological reflection understood that it was necessary to distinguish *hypostasis* from *ousia* in God. At the human level, however, there is evidently still equivalence, for every human person is a distinct substance with respect to other human persons. In Boethius' definition, if distinction is bound to substantiality, then the dimension of communion is brought back to the rational nature in that it is precisely the reason and the word that allow for the possibility of entering into relation.

In the twelfth century, Richard of St. Victor (†1173) exposed the limits of the Boethian definition. Though correct when applied to man, it breaks down when applied to God who is three Persons but not three substances. This is why Richard formulated a new definition: *incommunicable existence proper to the divine nature* (*De Trinitate*, IV, 22). So as to overcome the problem of Boethius' definition, he replaces substance with existence, referring this term, according to its etymology (*ex-sistentia*), to the being *from* (*ex*) another. Thus, the existence of the Father would consist of his not being from anyone, that of the Son would consist of being from the Father, and that of the Holy Spirit of being from the two first divine Persons. In this way, the noun used—*existence*—makes direct reference to communion and relation whereas the adjective *incommunicable* guarantees the distinction. This definition was a clear step forward, but it also had an obvious limit. It could be applied only to God because the existence of human persons is not like that of God in Whom each Person is exclusively distinct by His relation of origin in the other Persons of the Trinity, yet still identified with the single substance. The additional specification *unique to the divine nature* was necessary to avoid every possible misunderstanding. The definition, then, cannot be applied to man but only to the Trinity.

Ultimately, it is Thomas Aquinas who offers a definition that can be applied to both the creature and the Creator. He modifies Boethius' definition in the following way: The person is *the subsistent of a rational nature* (*ST* I, 29, a. 3, *ad* 3). Substance is replaced by the present participle of the verb *to subsist*, a verb that means 'to have one's own being in oneself'. This is why the definition is appropriate to the divine Persons, who are identified with the one substance that is Being itself, and therefore have no accidents. In this way, Thomas expresses what Boethius intended, though without using the term *substance,* which cannot be said of God in the plural. Furthermore, the use of the verb in its present participle refers directly to the subject of an action that in God is eternal. Obviously, when we speak about man, the dimension of eternity is not present, even though the definition applies to him perfectly.

Thus, Aquinas' theology succeeded in finding a formulation that is extended analogically to different levels of being, thus displaying the continuity between God and His image. Clearly, the divine Persons have subsistence in a perfect way to the extent of being identified with their relation of origin. Therefore, with respect to the Trinity, Aquinas' definition can be combined with another, which applies only to the Father, Son and Holy Spirit: The divine Person, is, in fact, *relation inasmuch as it is subsistent* (*ST* I,

29, a. 4, *ad* 3). If on the level of creation relation is an accident, in God it obviously is not, and is instead identified with the fullness of Being. This step forward is possible because relation is a pure reference to another reality that does not of itself modify the substance. So the Father is Fatherhood and in Him there is nothing else: The first Person does not give merely something to the other two, but gives Himself and is identified with the divine substance precisely in being the eternal source of this gift of Himself, of the gift of His divinity. So, too, is the Son none other than Sonship. Therefore, He is the divine substance received as a gift from the Father and given back to Him. And in this total giving back the gift of Himself the second Person is the image of the first. Lastly, the Holy Spirit is pure Spiration, that is, divine substance in being the eternal Gift that the Father and Son exchange between themselves.

Within man, the relationship between substance and relation is different than what it is with God. Whereas in the Trinity the Person refers directly to the relation and only indirectly to the substance, for us *person* points to substance in the first place and then, only indirectly, to relation. This is due to the imperfection of man who is called to become divinized by the Holy Spirit that he might grow in the image and likeness of God. This is something that anyone might experience by contemplating the saints, who were gradually identified with their relation to God and who gave their lives in love. This is demonstrated through the same bond of ultimate love that a person shows by giving his life for his friends, as Christ indicated in his farewell discourse during the Last Supper as the meaning of his life and the Paschal Mystery (*John* 15:13). This is not something merely moral. Instead, it is a journey towards full identity with the incarnate Son who came into the world to draw man into the Most Blessed Trinity and so bestow upon him eternal life. Man does not lose himself in giving himself, opening himself and allowing himself to enter into relation with the other, even if this means allowing himself to be wounded to stay true to that relation. For Being, the source of every being and every life, is relation.

Fatherhood and Sonship

The fundamental importance of the relational dimension was also grasped by the phenomenological research of the last century, and in unexpected areas of inquiry. For example, in an explicitly non-Christian context, psychoanalysis traces psychological pathologies back to an origin in wounds at the level of a person's fundamental relations. In order to understand man, one must begin from the fact of his being son.

It is essential, therefore, to know the Father and the Son and contemplate them more fully. The Trinity is not an abstract reality, a complex theological doctrine far removed from us. Rather, it is the source of our very being as well as our deepest aspirations. We are from the Trinity and for the Trinity. The bosom of the Father is our home and the ultimate source of our identity, for from Him stems all fatherhood in heaven and on earth (*Eph* 3:14–15).

In fact, the Father is the divine Person who is the origin and source of everything. The Son and the Spirit have their origin from Him in eternity, and that is why creation, which is the work of the whole Trinity, also has its ultimate origin in the plan of the Father. He is Origin without origin. According to the Athanasian creed, He *was neither made by anyone, nor created, nor generated.* Inasmuch as He is the source of fullness, the first Person is the true foundation of divine unity. One could say that calling God one *because* He is triune is tantamount to saying that God is one *because* He is Father. In fact, being Father implies the existence of a Son and the being bound to Him by Love. It is here that one sees the ontological newness represented by the personal and relational dimension, known to us only through revelation.

The fatherhood of the first Person is absolute in the sense that He is infinitely Father. That is why he is fully involved in the generation of the Son. He never existed without the Son. He did not *become* a Father, He *is* Father, pure and eternal relation to the Son and His Love. Moreover, he is so fully Father that he alone generates an Only-Begotten Son who, in turn, is perfectly identified with His very same divinity, with the divine substance.

The Son is fully Son: In Him there exists only the eternal receiving of Himself from the Father and the eternal orientation toward the Father. The second Person is pure *being from* and *being for* the Father, according to a beautiful expression of J. Ratzinger (*Introduction to Christianity*, Ignatius Press, San Francisco 2004, pp. 186–189). The Son is always perfectly and continually generated in eternity, without this implying imperfection or movement from potency to act but only fullness and depth of relation with the Father. The very use of the passive to indicate *being generated* is due to the limitations of our language, for in itself the Son's being generated is active and not passive. In God, to receive is not something "to which one is subjected", but the welcoming of a gift, a welcoming that constitutes the Giving as such. The language of gift helps because even among humans accepting a present is an active process. The same can be said for call and answer. Thus, the Father is Father because He generates the Son, but is also the Father because the Son accepts the Gift and, in a way that we are unable to express adequately, it is precisely the Son who makes the first Person Father. Hence, their relationship is an eternal gift of self, which, on the part of the Father, possesses the characteristics of origin and source while, on the part of the Son, it is an eternal giving-back of the Gift.

Hence, the Son is also called the image of the Father (*Col* 1:15, *Heb* 1:3). Just as the Father gives of Himself, so also the Son is His image precisely in the giving-back of Himself to the Father. He does not keep the Gift but gives of His own self to the Father in return. Though He is Life, He does live alone. Rather, He places Himself back in the hands of the source of Life.

This is also expressed in the name *the Word,* which is attributed to the second Person. Yet this name adds the reference to the purely spiritual dimension of the generation. This procession is analogous to the cognitive act of man because man too when he knows something has within himself, in his interior, an image of the known object. When man knows himself, the image that he forms of himself is intimate to the man himself and in an imperfect way is that man. Obviously, in God, the thought He has of Himself in knowing Himself is not only a concept. This thought is God Himself because here the act of knowing is utterly perfect. The Son is, then, the Thought of the Father. Clearly, this is only an analogy inasmuch as in man the concept that he forms is accidental and linked to the need to know, whereas in the Trinity it is the fruit of a perfect act of pure cognitive fertility.

Insistence on the Gift of Self is essential in understanding the significance of the new reality that has been revealed. There is no longer any sense in the image of God standing on high and determining all things by necessity. In that case, the identity of all that has its origin from Him would be an imposition and hence a mark of inferiority. Thus, in Christian reflection, it proved difficult initially to express the perfect divinity of the second divine Person. The Father and the Son are indeed God, the one and the same God, in eternal and reciprocal self-giving. The Father is not Father alone but rather in relation to the Son, and the Son is Himself in relation to the Father. Their identities are relational.

At this point, one can glimpse a reflection of the development of man and of his becoming aware of himself as son. When a child is small, he normally perceives only the perfection of his own parents, a perfection that is his first notion of the image of God. This happens because the world of the young is limited to the security of the home and family. However, he develops little by little and enters into relation with the external world. At the same time, he recognizes both his own limitations and the limitations of his parents, from whom his own limitations often derive. In this phase, one's own identity is often perceived as an imposition and generally receives adolescent rejection, accompanied by the need to appear different. In a certain sense, the fundamental relationship with parents is understood in a dialectical sense, because a person does not manage to accept his own limitations. The simple fact of the matter is that when a person enters the world he does not choose his father or his mother. In this sense, the relation is not totally free. However, with the onset of the adolescent crisis, combined with external confrontation, the child can gradually discover, beyond the limitations, the positive side of his family baggage, of his heritage, and can actually freely choose his own parents in accepting their limitations. This kind of *forgiveness* of one's father makes relation free and reciprocal; and from this gift, which is the essence of forgiveness, is also born the true identity of the son who, in accepting the limitations of his father, also accepts his own limitations and recognizes himself as a gift. The son is thus ready to become a father, that is, ready to give back to another the gift that he has received. And the same is true for a daughter.

Clearly, there are neither limits nor temporal sequence in the Trinity, but the relation of Father and Son is an eternal and reciprocal Gift of Self that is reflected in the image and likeness of the creature. For this reason, man becomes all the more easily son—that is, he overcomes the crisis of adolescent identity—the more he realizes that his father truly gives of himself, that he accepts his limitations and loves the world, despite the difficulties.

The Spirit and Love

This constant reference to the Gift of Self in speaking of the relation between the Father and the Son refers to the Holy Spirit, for

He is also known by the names Gift and Love. Speaking about Him is difficult because human language is too impoverished—one saint described him as the *Great Unknown* (J. Escrivá de Balaguer, *Christ Is Passing By,* New York: Scepter, 1974). This difficulty is bound up with His personal identity inasmuch as He expresses the mystery of the intimacy of God, similar to the way the spirit of man gives an indication of what is deepest in him. Moreover, His mission is totally directed toward the Son to whom he constantly refers. The Spirit does not speak of Himself, but only of the Son.

The very symbols that allude to Him in Scripture reveal His relationship with the second divine Person: For example, the baptismal water which flowed out together with blood from the pierced heart of Jesus (*Jn* 19:34), or the source of living water mentioned in the encounter with the woman of Samaria (*Jn* 4:10–14). The same can be said of the anointing and the seal which both refer directly to Christ whose name means *anointed one*. Again, one thinks of the cloud of the Transfiguration (*Lk* 9:34–35), the shadow of the Spirit at the Annunciation (*Lk* 1:35), and the fire with which Christ came to baptize (*Lk* 3:16).

Just as the generation of the Son is analogically related to knowledge, theology similarly draws a connection between the procession of the Spirit, technically termed Spiration, and the will and love. This corresponds to his being the bond that unites the Father and the Son, their very communion (cf. Augustine, *De Trinitate*, XV, 19, 37).

In fact, when someone knows something of reality he forms a concept of it that he keeps inside his mind and his interiority. A reality that is known can be desired; the will can orient a person toward it. Someone who has never seen pizza or ice cream cannot desire them. Advertizing operates on this principle. Thus, just as what is known is in the knower, so is what is loved in the lover. The will, however, has one peculiarity compared with the intellect in that the act of willing has a unifying force: If I know something bad, I do not become bad, whereas if I want something bad there is a change in me on the ontological level that renders me bad. I become what I desire; I am united to it. In a certain sense, this is a symmetrical movement with respect to what occurs in the process of thought that takes up the known in the knower. Indeed, the lover not only has the beloved within himself, but the lover also goes outside of himself and becomes one with the beloved. Love, therefore, unites and creates relation.

In the Trinity, by analogy, the Spirit proceeds as the Love of the Father for the Son and of the Son for the Father. He is the Person who joins and unites Them. One might say He is the Person of Communion and the Person of Relation, the bond of mutual Love. It is through Him, Spirit of the Father and Spirit of the Son, that the three Persons are reciprocally One in the Other.

This reality is known by the technical term *perichoresis,* which originally indicated a circular movement similar to a carousel. He who sees the Son sees the Father, Jesus says to Philip (*Jn* 14:8–9). So, the three Persons are one in the other because Each is identified with the divine substance. However, this is founded precisely in the third Person as eternal Gift and mutual Love that renders the Father and the Son a single reality.

On this point, there is disagreement between the Western and Eastern traditions, a disagreement linked to the Latin translation of the Nicene-Constantinopolitan Creed. In fact, in a theological context that recognized the Spirit as the bond of Love between the Father and the Son, the expression *and the Son* was added to the expression *proceeds from the Father* in the third article of the Creed in order to emphasize further the divinity of the second Person. The former expression is called the *Filioque* in Latin, from which derives the name of the dispute that led to the Great Schism of 1054. On two occasions, in two councils—Lyons in 1274 and

Florence in 1439—an agreement was reached, but neither was to last.

The texts of Scripture are restrained but clear. The Spirit proceeds (*ekporéuei*) from the Father (*Jn* 15:26). The Spirit takes from the Son and reveals what the Son has received from the Father (*Jn* 16:13–15). Jesus is the bearer of the Spirit (*Lk* 4:18), and the Son gives and sends the Spirit (*Jn* 15:26 and 20:22–23). On the basis of these passages, it is clear that throughout history, in the work of salvation, the third Person is sent by the second. The question is whether or not this corresponds to an intra-Trinitarian relation. We thereby return to the notion of how the relationships between the Trinity and the world are conceived.

Essentially, the problem stems from the fact that no equivalent verb exists in Latin to match the Greek term used to identify the procession of the Holy Spirit from the Father. As has been seen, Gregory Nazianzus coined the name of the second procession from the verb *ekporéutai,* which appears in John 15:26. In Greek, this refers to the Father as the Origin or Principle of the Trinity as a whole, in the same way as the Latin term *principaliter* introduced by Augustine. Therefore, in reading the Latin addition *and from the Son*, the Greeks were compelled to think that the Latin writers were claiming that the Spirit has two different origins, the Father and the Son, thus violating the monarchy. According to the railroad example, the terms used by the Latin writers were understood by the Greeks not as reference to a train that comes from New York via St. Louis, but to a train coming from to different starting points, which would be absurd. On the other hand, the Latin verb (*procedere*) used in the translation is generic and does not indicate the act of proceeding as from the first point of origin. Hence, it might not express the fact that the Son gives the Spirit back to the Father, that same Spirit who initially receives His origin from the Father, the Father Who is origin and source of all the Trinity. These problems of translation, which, until the eighth century, did not constitute a difficulty insofar as the various Greek and Latin theologians understood both languages, were compounded with complications related to political questions during the reign of Charlemagne in the 8th century and the relationship between the West and the East.

From a purely theological perspective, a first step was taken to clarify—at the Council of Lyons in 1274—that the Spirit proceeds from the Father and from the Son *as from a single principle* or *origin* in such a way that the monarchy of the Father is not compromised. However, this unity of the Father and the Son might be thought of as something merely essential, that is, as if it were based on substance and not on personal communion. This risks framing the relationship of the Father and the Son as a closed reality, disconnected from the third Person. In 1995, the Pontifical Council for the Promotion of Christian Unity published a clarification entitled *The Procession of the Holy Spirit in the Greek and Latin Traditions* in which it is explained how the Latin translation of the Creed does not contradict the monarchy of the Father. Moreover, the *Catechism of the Catholic Church* in paragraph 248 says that the Spirit proceeds from the Father *as Father of the Only-Begotten Son*. To be more precise, the first Person is the origin of the third Person precisely because he is Father. But this implies the presence of the Son, for the Father is such only for the Son.

In a certain way, the dispute over the *Filioque* highlights the importance of relation and of how communion is endangered when it lacks a shared language and experience of life. It also underscores the need to deepen the study of how the Trinitarian revelation influences our worldview. In fact, it is precisely at the pneumatological level where one sees the clearest indication of the newness of the Trinitarian conception of God, of Being and of the world.

In the ancient view, the First Principle did not have relations at all, otherwise it would no longer be Absolute (*ab-solutus*)—that is, it would no longer be set apart, separated and free of all ties. To have relations implied inferiority and difference with respect to the first principle. For this very reason, the mediator figures were always marked by imperfection, as was seen in the difficulty of recognizing the perfect divinity of Christ in the third and fourth centuries.

Instead, the triune God is a Father who is eternally Himself through the act of generation, that is, in the giving of Himself to the Son; and the latter is the image of the Father in giving Himself back to the Father. Just as the Father gives Himself, the Son gives Himself back in return. In its absolute depth, Being is a giving back of the gift. The Father is not the Father by himself, but in his Love for the Son, in generating him eternally; and the Son is not God by himself, but in the giving back of Himself through Love to the Father; and the Love, the Holy Spirit, is the very relation that unites the Father and the Son and renders Them Father and Son. The two processions cannot be considered independent and separate, just as, analogically, knowledge and love refer to each other in a reciprocal way.

From this there follows a new vision of the relationship between God and the world. In fact, the triune God has no need to protect Himself; rather, He is so great that he can make Himself small. He can send the Son to become a man through Love, that is, through the Holy Spirit. God is relation and therefore has relations. God is gift and therefore gives of Himself. He gives of Himself without losing Himself because He is the infinite source of Good. This is difficult to grasp on account of original sin inasmuch as original sin always leads one to think of the finite, to contemplate in the light of the fear of losing. However, God thinks of the infinite, and this loving thought is the Son. Authentic transcendence is that which is capable not only of remaining beyond (*trans-*) but also of *descending among,* according to a beautiful expression of Pierpaolo Donati (*La matrice teologica della società,* Rubbettino, Soveria Mannelli 2010, page 93). The washing of the feet and Peter's reaction to Jesus' kneeling down perfectly demonstrates man's bewilderment in the face of a *Logos* who is, as Thomas wrote, the *Word that breathes forth Love* (*ST* I, 43, a. 5), a *Logos Who is simultaneously a lover with all the passion of true love* (Benedict XVI, *Deus Caritas Est*, n. 11). Humility itself, which was not considered a virtue in classical culture, becomes a distinctive mark of divinity because every Person of the Trinity is Himself through the others. Every Person is not alone, but in relation.

From this bewilderment in the face of the Trinitarian *logic* of God is born a vision of the world as a meeting place with God, of work as service to man and praise to the Lord, of the search for truth as dialogue, and of the Christian apostolate as friendship. From this conception of transcendence, which not only remains *above* history but also desires to be *within* it—in a union without confusion—there also grows a positive vision of the secular, and the autonomy of created reality. Man is a son and not a servant, and God enters into authentic dialogue with him, respecting man's liberty to the extreme that ultimately brings Him to endure the Cross.

The key, therefore, is divine sonship: The Holy Spirit renders man a son in the Son, the image of this Trinitarian God, an image not on its own, but in its relations. As a result, and not just because of moral demands, the family is central and has a metaphysical value. Friendship and human love are thus essential to life. The very being of man springs from the Love of the Trinity and is fulfilled only by returning to this Love, which brings every person back to the Father in Christ. The unity of the God who is one because He is triune must be communicated to all so that they can be in communion with one another in the manner of the divine Persons: *That they may all be one, just as you, Father, are in me, and I in you, that they also may be in us* (*Jn* 17:21).

The Trinity Throughout History: Missions and Indwelling

This unity in God is the purpose of the missions. Irenaeus described the Son and the Spirit as the hands of the Father. They enter into the world to embrace the whole of history and bring everything back to the Father. The study of the missions is the culmination of Trinitarian doctrine, which links it with all the other theological treatises, from ecclesiology to eschatology, from the sacraments to grace.

On reading the New Testament, it is clear that the second and third Persons are sent into the world. They are both often referred to by the verbs "to give" and "to send": "For God so loved the world, that he gave his only begotten Son, that whoever believes in him should not perish but have eternal life. For God did not send his Son into the world to condemn the world, but in order that the world might be saved through him" (*Jn* 3:16–17); "And I will ask the Father, and he will give you another Helper" (*Jn* 14:16); "But the Helper, the Holy Spirit, whom the Father will send in my name, he will teach you all things and bring to your remembrance all that I have said to you" (*Jn* 14:26).

Obviously, God is present in the world through his omnipresence, his immensity and because he sustains all things in being. The creature would not exist without the Creator. With the missions, however, the Son and the Spirit begin to be present in the world in a new way, in the human person, who is transformed. The gift of the missions communicates something of the personal characteristic of the Persons who have been sent. That is why, in Romans 8:15–16, we read that the Spirit cries out *Abbà* in the sons of God. Coming into the world, the Son and the Spirit wish to take everything to the Father, for His Fatherhood embraces every person. This is the self-giving of the Trinity to man, the presence of the Trinity throughout history because, through *perichoresis*, where there is one Person, there are all three.

97

The mission is, in fact, the extension of the eternal procession into the created world—*the mission includes the eternal procession and adds something else, namely, the effect of time* (*ST* I, 43, a. 2, ad 3). The Son and the Spirit are made known to us through their personal distinction, and so in Their origin with respect to the Father. For example, just as the Son receives Himself from the Father and gives back all of Himself to the Father, so too in the mission He receives and gives back all the world and its entire history to the Father, rendering Him all the glory. To sanctify one's own work, one's family and social life mean to live one's own divine sonship in its fullness in union with the mission of Christ who leads everything back to the Father. This is fulfilled in every Mass, when, at the end of the Eucharistic Prayer, the priest says: "Through him, and with him, and in him, O God almighty Father, in the unity of the Holy Spirit, all glory and honour is yours, for ever and ever."

The mission exists within time, but its foundation is in eternity. The Trinity is truly present in history. Obviously, the divine Persons do not change, nor are they separated from the Father. Nor is the Father ontologically superior to the Son or the Spirit who are sent. This is not equivalent to the case of a servant or an ambassador. The only changes are found in the human person who is the purpose of the missions: The recipient acquires a new relation with each of the Persons sent inasmuch as he is distinct from the other two. The history of salvation becomes the salvation of history because time is truly united to the eternal.

When the mission is accompanied by visible signs, as in the Incarnation and Pentecost, it is called visible. When, instead, there is no external sign, the mission is called *invisible*, like the indwelling of the Holy Spirit in the soul of the righteous (*Rom* 5:5, *Gal* 4:4–6, *1 Cor* 3:16–17). The purpose of the missions, therefore, is sanctification, the embrace of love between human beings and the three divine Persons.

The indwelling of the Trinity itself is the end or objective of the divine missions and the aim of all creation: A relation of mutual presence between the divine Persons and human beings, which is realized in a dialogue of knowledge and love. In this way, God Himself dwells within man, or, more accurately, God possesses man to such a degree that God causes man to dwell in Him.

Scripture speaks of this clearly: "If anyone loves me, he will keep my word, and my Father will love him, and we will come to him and make our home with him" (*Jn* 14:23); the Spirit is sent to the disciples (see *Jn* 15:26, 16:7, *Gal* 4:6); the Spirit who raised Jesus from the dead dwells in Christians (*Rom* 8:11), and charity is the gift of the Spirit who cries out *Abbà* in our hearts (*Rom* 8:15); the bodies of the Christians are called "temples" of the Spirit, analogously with how God dwelt in the temple of Jerusalem (*1 Cor* 3:16–17). This indwelling is the fulfilment of a long tradition in the Old Testament concerning the closeness of God to his people.

The Fathers of the Church gave a powerful description of the reality of this new presence of the Trinity in the soul, not as a simple metaphor or hyperbole but as an experience made possible by the action of the Holy Spirit. His is an authentic substantial presence that enables man to enter into relation with the three divine Persons, distinguishing the One from the Other. The acts of knowledge and love of the human soul are elevated to such a degree as to reach intimacy with God. This happens because the Spirit renders us sons in the Son: The divine sonship can be seen as the foundation of this indwelling, together with sanctifying grace and the theological virtues. Just as God is fully revealed to man in Christ, so He also causes us to dwell in Him through the sonship of Christ.

This implies a radical change within man, who becomes divinized and acquires a new kind of spontaneousness as well as a new vision of the world. Everything comes to be viewed through the eyes of Christ and His loving relation with the Father. The creation is thus transfigured: Matter and spirit can no longer be separated and nothing can be considered truly profane. Contemplation can no longer stop at the surface of things, at that unity which is also grasped in a way that is simply natural. Rather, it penetrates the depths of being until it recognizes that everything in the world and in everyday life speaks of the Trinity, until it tastes the authentic unity that rises from the intimate communion of the one and triune God.

This is possible, however, only with faith in the action of the Holy Spirit who can transform a heart of stone into a heart of flesh (*Ezek* 36:25–28), only if one lets himself be guided beyond the securities offered by the senses and the conceptions which harmonize with merely natural experience. One might say that the interior life of a person follows a path similar to the history of dogma that has been laid out in these pages. Just as, in the face of the revelation he has received, man has to gradually abandon the limited categories of his own thought in order to open himself to a new way of thinking purified by the experience of God, so too the soul must abandon the false securities of its own way of thinking about itself and the world in order to open itself without reserve to relation with the Father, the Son and the Holy Spirit.

6. Conclusion: Mary and the Trinity

We have seen that the indwelling of the Trinity constitutes the aim of the whole of creation, the fulfilment of the life of human beings. This claim finds its perfect realization in Mary who is the very pinnacle of creation. Vatican Council II speaks thus of her: "Redeemed, in a more exalted fashion, by reason of the merits of her Son and united to Him by a close and indissoluble tie, she is endowed with the high office and dignity of the Mother of the Son of God, and therefore she is also the beloved of the Father and the temple of the Holy Spirit. Because of this gift of sublime grace she far surpasses all creatures, both in heaven and on earth" (*Lumen gentium*, 53).

This text emphasizes how the divine Motherhood of Mary is the foundation of her relations with the three divine Persons, in Their unity and in Their distinction. Thus, in Mary the presence of the Trinity is realized to the highest degree, and no one is more fully immersed in the Trinity than she. Therefore, it is appropriate we speak about her before concluding the study of the doctrine of the one and triune God. As her greatness came to be gradually understood, one can see again the essential development of Trinitarian thought.

We have seen, in fact, that any reflection on the Trinity is tied to an increased understanding of the relationship between God and the world. Gradually, it was understood that God not only *has* relations but *is* three eternal Relations. The *Logos* is not a figure of ontological mediation between the Father and creation. Nor is He an intermediary who stands halfway between God and the world.

He is the eternal Son, eternally generated in the Love of the Holy Spirit. The distinction of the three divine Persons is not caused by a difference in Their essence but only by their relations of origin.

This progress of thought is reflected in the understanding of the relationship between the Trinity and creation, and, therefore, between the Trinity and she who is the crown of creation.

Initially, patristic texts placed a strong emphasis on the connection between Mary and the flesh of Christ: The humanity of Jesus originates from her. In the context of *Logos*-theology in which one is not yet able to express the intra-Trinitarian distinction in terms of relations because a theology of the natures has not yet been articulated, we observe an unfortunate consequence: The prerogatives of Mary cannot be affirmed in all their perfection. In fact, there was a fear that the Mother of God might be confused with God himself. Thus, while the virginity in childbirth is affirmed immediately so as to demonstrate the divinity of Jesus according to the prophecy of Emmanuel in Isaiah 7:14, there is uncertainty concerning her virginity after the birth of Christ. These doubts are still present in Origen in the third century. He also denies the perfect faith of Mary, interpreting the sword that will pierce her soul, prophesied by Simeon (*Lk* 2:35), as scandal and abandonment in the face of the death of her Son. This exegesis even has an influence on Basil.

During the fourth century, however, the situation changes. With the reflections of Gregory of Nyssa and Gregory Nazianzus, the virginity of Mary is reinterpreted according to the theological key of the attribute of Life, and thus traced directly to the eternal Virginity and Incorruptibility of the Father. The Father is such because He has the fullness of Life, and thus the Son who receives the fullness of this Life through generation is Virgin. Likewise, the third Person, who is the Spirit of Life, is Virgin. The perpetual virginity of Mary is interpreted departing from the relationship between Mary and the Trinity Itself (Gregory of Nyssa, *De verginitate,*

II). These authors unpack the title Mother of God (*Theotókos*), and her prerogatives are hereafter formulated in all their perfection. At the Council of Constantinople, in 381, Mary is inserted into the Creed professed by the entire Church.

The distinction between the one and only uncreated and eternal nature, which is the Trinity, and all other created natures allows the affirmation of union without fear of confusions. Distinction must no longer be connected with inferiority and imperfection. This applies to the Son, Who is consubstantial with the Father and is distinguished from the Father only through relation, and it also applies to the Mother of God, who has a different substance from the Trinity yet is united in a unique way to her Son in the singular and vital relation she has with Him. Moreover, in the Son, Mary is united with the whole Trinity. The mutual presence of indwelling is realized in her in a perfect and singular manner, both spiritual and physical, because the *Logos* is made flesh in her, and she, being assumed into Heaven both body and soul, is crowned Queen of the universe by the Trinity. She who offered the womb of her own body to the Son enters with her body into the bosom of the Father.

Just as the Son is perfect by nature and is God as pure *being from* the Father and *being for* the Father, so Mary is perfectly divinized by grace in being everything for the Son, as Virgin and Mother of God, and everything from the Son, as the Immaculate One. In this her pure relation to the Son are founded her relations to the Father and the Spirit.

Hence, the beautiful words that go back to Francis of Assisi, *Daughter of God the Father, Mother of God the Son, and Bride of God the Holy Spirit* (*Writings*, 163), are not merely a pious expression. They manifest the very being of Mary, her ontology, in which her essence is utterly filial and totally maternal. Mary lives in relations because she is pure relation, the pure transparency of God like the purest crystal. She is like the fire of the burning bush that makes the divine Fire present and visible.

It thus becomes possible for every person to *reach the Trinity of Heaven, through another trinity, that of the earth: Jesus, Mary and Joseph*, as was perceived by a saint of our own day (S. Bernal. *Josemaria Escriva de Balaguer: A Profile of the Founder of Opus Dei*, London: Scepter, 1977, 360). The unity of the God who is One because He is the triune God is communicated to man, to the family, to friendships and to daily life, divinizing them to the point that relations become the way we rise, through Mary, to the Father, through the Son, in the Holy Spirit.[10]

10 On October 11, 2010 to the Synod for the Middle East, Benedict XVI affirmed that Mary is the Mother of the Church precisely because she is the Mother of God, a God Who is relation and desires to draw all things to Himself. It is she who shows us that God is one *because* He is three.